SPIRITUAL
WARFARE
IN THE
END
TIMES

RON RHODES

HARVEST HOUSE PUBLISHERS
EUGENE, OREGON

Spiritual Warfare in the End Times
Copyright © 2020 by Ron Rhodes
Published by Harvest House Publishers
Eugene, Oregon 97408
www.harvesthousepublishers.com

ISBN 978-0-7369-8035-7 (pbk)
ISBN 978-0-7369-8036-4 (eBook)

Library of Congress Cataloging-in-Publication Data

Names: Rhodes, Ron, author.
Title: Spiritual warfare in the end times / Ron Rhodes.
Description: Eugene, OR : Harvest House Publishers, 2020. | Includes
    bibliographical references. | Summary: "Bible prophecy expert Ron Rhodes
    explores the tactics Satan uses to attack God's people, and what
    Scripture tells us about how to respond effectively-with the help of the
    Holy Spirit, angels, prayer, and more"-- Provided by publisher.
Identifiers: LCCN 2020006447 (print) | LCCN 2020006448 (ebook) | ISBN
    9780736980357 (trade paperback) | ISBN 9780736980364 (ebook)
Subjects: LCSH: Spiritual warfare. | End of the world.
Classification: LCC BV4509.5 .R478 2020 (print) | LCC BV4509.5 (ebook) |
    DDC 235/.4--dc23
LC record available at https://lccn.loc.gov/2020006447
LC ebook record available at https://lccn.loc.gov/2020006448

In loving memory of
Mark David Stout

Acknowledgments

Through the years I've received countless letters and e-mails from people around the world asking various questions about spiritual warfare. Thank you for taking the time to write. You are one reason I wrote this book.

During the writing of this book, my long-time friend Norman Geisler exited earthly life and entered heavenly glory. He was one of my primary mentors at Dallas Theological Seminary in the late 1970s and early 1980s. Little did I know as a seminary student that I would one day be doing conferences with him and even writing some books with him. I continue to be appreciative for all I've learned from him through the decades—including such doctrines as angelology and demonology. His legacy lives on in his many students.

I continue to be thankful to our gracious God for the wondrous gift of my family—Kerri, David, and Kylie. Without their endless love and support, my work of ministry would truly be an impossible task and wouldn't be near as fun.

Most of all, I want to express profound thanks and appreciation to our Lord Jesus Christ. It is such an honor and privilege to serve Him through the written word.

Thank You, Lord, for providing us all we need to know about spiritual warfare in Your Word.

Contents

Introduction: Spiritual Warfare. 7

Part 1: Understanding Your Enemy

1. The Reality of Satan in the World Today 21
2. The Character and Goal of Satan and His Fallen Angels 37
3. Understanding Spiritual Warfare 53

Part 2: Understanding Enemy Tactics

4. *Satan's Schemes:* Flaming Darts, Mind Games, Guilt,
   and Discouragement 69
5. *Satan's Schemes:* Depression, Doubts, Worry, Anger,
   Personal Offense, and Robbing Joy. 83
6. *Satan's Schemes:* Pride, Hindering Prayer, Sin,
   and Causing Division. 95
7. *Satan's Schemes:* Hindering Through Other People,
   Bodily Illness, Attacking Churches, and Apostasy. 107
8. *Satan's Schemes:* False Religions, Persecution,
   and Reducing Religious Freedom. .121

Part 3: Resisting and Defeating the Enemy

9. Our Position in Christ 135
10. The Role of the Holy Spirit 145
11. The Armor of God 159
12. The Role of Prayer. 171
13. The Role of Angels 183

Postscript 197
Appendix: Key Bible Verses on Our Position in Christ 205
Bibliography 207
Endnotes 213

Spiritual Warfare

Thank you for joining me in this exciting journey through God's Word. I wrote this book to help Christians understand what Scripture says about spiritual warfare, both now and into the prophetic end times. My hope and prayer is that as you read this book, you will attain...

- a better understanding of spiritual warfare and how knowledge of this warfare can benefit your life spiritually, emotionally, and even physically;

- an awareness—perhaps for the first time in your life—of the specific tactics Satan is most likely to use against you *this year* and the years that follow as we move into the end times;

- insights into the ways Satan can gain a stronghold in your life—as well as what you can do to prevent it *and* what you can do if he already has one;

- an understanding about the gang attack—composed of the world, the flesh, and the devil—that daily confronts you;

- an awareness of how satanic and demonic attacks will intensify in the end times, especially in the years that immediately precede the second coming of Christ;

- a strong conviction about how staying close to Jesus is one of the most important factors in your victory in spiritual warfare. (The sheep who are the safest from the wolves are those who stay nearest the Shepherd.) Jesus' victory becomes our victory;

- insights about the pivotal role of the Holy Spirit (the "Spirit of truth") in overcoming the devil (the "father of lies");

- an understanding of how to daily get dressed in God's armor, which will keep you safe in the trenches of spiritual warfare;

- a strong conviction about the strategic importance of prayer in overcoming the archenemy of our souls;

- a strong conviction about the strategic importance of God's Word in standing against—*and defeating*—the archenemy of our souls;

- insights about God's holy angels and how God uses these invisible secret agents behind the scenes to protect you and bring blessing into your life;

- an exalted view of the supreme majesty, glory, and power of Jesus Christ;

- a strong conviction that God will one day bring a

mighty triumph over all the powers of evil. That day may come sooner than you think!

Satan and Demons in the End Times

As we consider a who's who of important persons in the end times, we think about the antichrist, the false prophet, the 144,000 Jewish witnesses, and the two great prophets who manifest supernatural powers similar to those of Moses and Elijah. Less emphasized by many students of the prophetic Word are the roles of God's angels, Satan, and demons, even though their activities are pervasive in the end times.

Biblical prophecy reveals that satanic and demonic activities will increase as we progress toward the end times. As Mark Hitchcock puts it, "according to Scripture, demonic activity and spiritual warfare will increase dramatically in frequency and intensity during the end times (see Revelation 9)…We can expect demonic activity to ramp up as the end times draw near, and it appears that's just what's happening."[1]

Please allow me to give you a few end-time highlights from the pages of Scripture. First, did you know that a great angelic battle in the heavenlies will transpire at the midpoint of the tribulation period? It will be a sight to behold! Here's what Revelation 12:7-9 says about it:

> Now war arose in heaven, Michael and his angels fighting against the dragon. And the dragon and his angels fought back, but he was defeated, and there was no longer any place for them in heaven. And the great dragon was thrown down, that ancient serpent, who is called the devil and Satan, the deceiver of the whole world— he was thrown down to the earth, and his angels were thrown down with him.

Satan becomes ferocious at this turn of events. He immediately kicks into high gear. John speaks of a loud voice from heaven that describes the devil's wrathful fervor this way: "Woe to you, O earth and sea, for the devil has come down to you in great wrath, because he knows that his time is short!" (Revelation 12:12). Satan knows he now has only three and a half years before Jesus' glorious second coming, and therefore goes forth with a vengeance to do as much damage as he can on earth, especially against Jews and Christians.

Satan will work powerfully through the antichrist during the tribulation period. Revelation 13:2 tell us that Satan will give the antichrist "his power and his throne and great authority." Second Thessalonians 2:9 likewise informs us: "The coming of the lawless one [the antichrist] is by the activity of Satan with all power and false signs and wonders." This means that the antichrist will be virtually energized by the devil, and for that reason, *the character of the antichrist will reflect that of the devil*. Two examples will suffice:

1. The Antichrist Deceives the Same Way Satan Does. We learn from Scripture that Satan is the "father of lies" (John 8:44). He originates and inspires lies and deception. In fact, Satan is a master deceiver and the greatest among all liars. His lies are often religious, distorting the biblical picture of God, Jesus, and the true gospel. Satan is "the deceiver of the whole world" (Revelation 12:9).

Because Satan is the father of lies and the deceiver of the whole world, it makes sense that the one he energizes—the antichrist— will also be full of lies and deception. Scripture reveals that the antichrist will engage in "all wicked deception for those who are perishing" (2 Thessalonians 2:10). A major aspect of his deception is that he engages in "false signs and wonders," exalting himself before a watching world (2 Thessalonians 2:9). People will be duped into thinking the antichrist must be "God among us," thereby mimicking the miracle-working Christ who *truly was* God among us (Matthew 1:23).

The antichrist will be full of poisonous, lethal deception. Satan will meanwhile be busy blinding the minds of unbelievers so they cannot perceive the truth (2 Corinthians 4:4). With such Satan-induced blindness, it is easy to understand how unbelievers will fall for the self-exalting claims of the antichrist (2 Thessalonians 2:9-11).

2. The Antichrist Persecutes the Same Way Satan Does. In Revelation 12:12-17, we find a sobering description of Satan's ousting from heaven, after which he engages in relentless persecution against the Jews. In parallel fashion, the antichrist will also be a great persecutor of the Jews. Daniel 9:27 tells us that the tribulation period will begin when the antichrist makes a covenant with the Jewish people. He will then break this covenant midway through the tribulation, at which point he will take "his seat in the temple of God, proclaiming himself to be God" (2 Thessalonians 2:4). This will utterly desolate the Jewish temple (Matthew 24:15). When this happens, the Jews in Jerusalem will need to escape from the city. Jesus prophetically warns:

> Let those who are in Judea flee to the mountains. Let the one who is on the housetop not go down to take what is in his house, and let the one who is in the field not turn back to take his cloak. And alas for women who are pregnant and for those who are nursing infants in those days! Pray that your flight may not be in winter or on a Sabbath. For then there will be great tribulation, such as has not been from the beginning of the world until now, no, and never will be (Matthew 24:16-21).

The antichrist's persecution of the Jews will be relentless. There will be countless casualties (Jeremiah 30:7; Zechariah 13:8).

We might say, in summary, that the antichrist—energized by Satan—will be Satan's CEO on the earth during the tribulation period. A chief executive officer carries the authority of leadership in an organization, and he implements the vision of the organization. The antichrist will head up Satan's evil enterprise in a seven-year reign of terror, using perpetual lies, fraud, deceit, theft, abuse of power, duplicity, self-interest, self-aggrandizement, persecution, and murder—*all under Satan's power*. We'll consider details throughout the rest of this book.

Satan and Demons in the Present Age

Christ's parables in Matthew 13 describe the course of the present age—the period that spans Christ's first and second comings, in which we now live. The theological backdrop is that Christ offered the kingdom to the Jews (Matthew 11–12). However, the Jewish leaders not only rejected Jesus but even claimed He performed miracles not in the power of the Holy Spirit but in the power of Satan, the *un*holy spirit. The Jewish leaders' monumental rejection of Christ, the Jewish Messiah, is the reason for the judicial blindness and hardening that has come upon Israel as a judgment from God (Romans 11:25).

God's kingdom program was thereby put on hold—its establishment was delayed. It will remain delayed until Christ's future one-thousand-year millennial kingdom, which follows the second coming.

Meanwhile, Jesus in Matthew 13 reveals what the course of the present age will be like. Briefly:

The parable of the sower teaches that this age will feature the sowing of the gospel seed onto different types of soil (Matthew 13:1-23).

The meaning is that people will have varying responses to the gospel—some good, some bad, some mixed.

The parable of the weeds reveals that when the gospel seed is planted around the world, there will also be a false countersowing by an "enemy" (Matthew 13:24-30,36-43). Only a judgment following the future tribulation period will separate the wheat (true believers) from the weeds (unbelievers or false believers).

The parable of the mustard seed reveals that God's spiritual kingdom would have an almost imperceptible beginning—hardly even noticeable. But just as a small mustard seed can produce a large plant (it can grow over fifteen feet high), so God's spiritual kingdom would start small but grow to be very large (Matthew 13:31-32).

Bible scholars interpret *the parable of the leaven* variously (Matthew 13:33). Most believe that in Scripture, leaven typically represents evil (see Matthew 16:12; Mark 8:15; Luke 12:1; 1 Corinthians 5:6-8; Galatians 5:9). They conclude that the parable means that false teaching may emerge and grow exponentially and even penetrate Christendom by the time of Christ's second coming.

Bible scholars also interpret *the parable of the hidden treasure* variously (Matthew 13:44). Many believe Jesus was pointing to the incredible value of the true kingdom of heaven as opposed to counterfeit belief systems. Those who truly see its importance will do anything within their power to possess it.

We can discern the work of the devil in several of these parabolic word pictures provided by our Lord:

- People can have different responses to the gospel because various forces are opposed to the gospel, including the world, the flesh, and the devil (see John 15:19; Romans 7:18; 8:7; 13:14; Galatians 5:16-17; 1 John 2:15-17).

- There will be a false countersowing by an "enemy" leading to the growth of "weeds" (unbelievers or false believers) (see 2 Corinthians 4:4; Ephesians 2:2-3). There is no greater enemy to the gospel than Satan.

- False teaching may emerge and grow exponentially and penetrate Christendom—no doubt rooted in "teachings of demons" (1 Timothy 4:1) and false prophets inspired by the devil (1 John 4:1-3).

- Standing against the exponential growth of God's kingdom, Satan through the antichrist will seek to set up a counterfeit kingdom on earth during the tribulation period (Revelation 13).

In view of all this, my goal in this book is to address spiritual warfare not only as related to the more distant end times but also (especially) as related to the present age. In a number of cases, we will see that Satan's work in the present age will directly escalate—coming to full fruition during the future tribulation period.

For example, even now Satan inspires false prophets, and this is preparing for the rise of the ultimate false prophet during the tribulation period (Revelation 13:11-18; 16:13; 19:20; 20:10). Even now Satan inspires false Christs in the kingdom of the cults, and this is preparing for the rise of the ultimate false Christ during the tribulation period—the antichrist (Revelation 13:1-10; 2 Thessalonians 2:9). Even now Satan inspires false religions, and this is setting the stage for the ultimate false religion in the tribulation period—the one-world religion associated with New Babylon (Revelation 17). Even now God's people are experiencing significant spiritual warfare (Ephesians 6:10-18), and this is setting the stage for the great escalation of spiritual warfare in the tribulation period (see Revelation 12:4-6,12-13; 13:7).

Nothing to Fear

Though this book deals with a serious and sobering subject, my prayer is that you will find it educational, enriching, and even exciting—especially in view of the complete victory we have in Jesus Christ. Because of that victory, you and I need not experience fear when we study this subject.

Someone once said that if you have a proper fear of (or *reverence* for) the Lord, you need not fear anyone (or anything) else. Conversely, if you lack fear of the Lord, then there's plenty you ought to be fearful of. In view of this reality, each of us should center all that we do in Jesus Christ—including all the battles we face in spiritual warfare. Staying near (and *reverencing*) the divine Shepherd is the single safest place for a sheep in an environment full of hungry wolves.

As you study this book, never forget that our God is an awesome God whose sovereign plan is now unfolding in human history. God Himself asserts, "As I have planned, so shall it be, and as I have purposed, so shall it stand" (Isaiah 14:24). In view of such scriptural facts, Robert Lightner—one of my favorite mentors from back in seminary days—advises each of us:

> When viewed from the perspective of Scripture, history is more than the recording of the events of the past. Rather, what has happened in the past, what is happening now, and what will happen in the future is all evidence of the unfolding of the purposeful plan devised by the personal God of the Bible. All the circumstances of life—past, present, and future—is all evidence of the unfolding of the purposeful plan devised by the personal God of the Bible. All the circumstances of life—past, present, and future—fit into the sovereign plan like pieces of a puzzle.[2]

In like manner, C.S. Lewis famously said that "history is a story written by the finger of God." God controls nations (Job 12:23-24; Psalm 22:28; Jeremiah 27:5-6; Daniel 4:17), sets up kings and deposes them (Daniel 2:21), and does all according to His sovereign plan (Acts 4:27-28). Our God is an awesome God, and He is in ultimate control—over humans, angels, Satan, and demons. That is cause to rejoice!

Despite what Satan and demons would like to do to us today, and despite what they will in fact do during the future tribulation period, *God is yet in control of all things.* Never forget it. He is guiding human history toward its culmination, and for that reason we have nothing to fear. *Ever!*

An Exhortation

In this book you will learn about Satan's ability as "the tempter." He is very effective at it. This is why the apostle Paul, greatly concerned for the Christians in Thessalonica, wrote to them: "When I could bear it no longer, I sent to learn about your faith, for fear that somehow the tempter had tempted you and our labor would be in vain" (1 Thessalonians 3:5).

In view of Satan's effectiveness as a tempter, I give you a frank word of warning that he will seek to tempt you not to read this book. He may seek to distract you with the idea that there are more important matters to attend to right now. Or that it might just be better (and more fun) to watch television. He might tempt you with the idea that this subject is not important or that it's too dark a subject to want to study. He might tempt you to not waste your time on it.

Do not fall for his tempting tactics (Ephesians 6:11).

I urge you to not only make a commitment to read this entire book, but also pray that the Lord will protect your time in reading it. I promise you'll be better off in your spiritual life if you read it all the way through to the end.

Here's another word of warning: Once you've read the book, Satan will likely tempt you to keep what you've learned as head knowledge rather than to put what you've learned into action. If this happens, then you are just as easy prey as you were before you read the book. Do not let that happen. I urge you to ask God to help you put into action what you learn. Here's a prayer I use regularly:

> Lord, I ask You to open my eyes and enhance my understanding so I can grasp what You want me to learn today (Psalm 119:18). I recognize that my time is a gift from You and that I am a steward of how I use it (Ephesians 5:15; Colossians 4:5). That being so, I ask You to protect my time as I seek to read this book (Philippians 4:6). Please give me discernment to recognize the tactics of the enemy in seeking to distract me (1 Peter 5:8). I also ask You to enable me, by Your Spirit, to apply the truths I learn to my daily life (Galatians 5:16-23) and guide me moment by moment by Your Word (Psalm 119:105; 2 Timothy 3:15-17). I thank You in Jesus' name. Amen.

PART 1

UNDERSTANDING YOUR ENEMY

We do not wrestle against flesh and blood,
but against the rulers, against the authorities,
against the cosmic powers
over this present darkness,
against the spiritual forces of evil
in the heavenly places.

(EPHESIANS 6:12)

The Reality of Satan in the World Today

A big problem for many of us is that we base everything on what our five senses tell us. Since the spiritual world is not subject to any of these, we often act as if it does not exist.

The eye of faith can perceive this unseen reality (Hebrews 11:1). The spiritual world lies all about us, enclosing us, embracing us, altogether within our reach. This spiritual world will come alive to us the moment we reckon upon its reality. Unfortunately, this spiritual world is brimming with not only benevolent spirit entities (God and His holy angels) but also malevolent spirit entities (Satan and his fallen angels, or demons).

We find many examples of the spirit world in the pages of Scripture. In 2 Kings 6:8-23, for example, we read of how Elisha found himself surrounded by enemy troops, yet he remained calm and relaxed. His servant, however, panicked at the sight of this hostile army with vicious-looking warriors and innumerable battle chariots on every side.

Undaunted, Elisha said to him, "Do not be afraid, for those who are with us are more than those who are with them" (2 Kings 6:16). Elisha then prayed, "'O LORD, please open his eyes that he may see.' So the LORD opened the eyes of the young man, and he saw, and behold, the mountain was full of horses and chariots of fire all around Elisha" (verse 17). God was protecting Elisha and his servant with a whole army of magnificent angelic beings!

I've often wondered if Elisha and other great prophets of God could also perceive Satan and demons as easily as Elisha could perceive God's angels. Regardless, one thing is certain. Satan's modus operandi today is to operate incognito. He does not want his presence known or detected. He prefers to engage in his devious deeds by stealth.

Denying or Redefining Satan

There are many denials of Satan's existence today. Modern psychology rests upon the foundation of secularism and humanism, worldviews that deny the supernatural. This means most psychologists deny the existence of a literal Satan and demons.

It is ironic that psychologists often refer to a person's "demons." By this they do not mean to express belief in wicked spirits. They use the term to describe specific psychological issues that a patient needs to resolve.

Liberal Christian scholars, who say the Bible is a manmade book, also deny the existence of Satan. Like humanistic psychologists, they have an antisupernatural bias. They often say belief in Satan and demons is part of the mythology from which the biblical writers borrowed when they wrote Scripture. They conclude that Satan and demons are nothing but legend and lore.

Such liberal scholars assert that there is no place for mythology in the modern world. A national poll of five thousand American clergymen—almost all of them liberal—found that 73 percent ridiculed the concept of a personal devil of any sort.

The famous liberal scholar Elaine Pagels, in her book *The Origin of Satan*, claims belief in Satan emerged around 150 BC among dissident Jews such as the Essenes at Qumran.[1] She claimed that some followers of Jesus also accepted the belief. These, too, she says, were "dissident Jews." She concludes that the idea of Satan became a means of interpreting human conflict or characterizing human enemies.

Some modern New Age leaders, such as David Spangler, suggest there is no literal evil being known as Satan, for everything in the universe is God (Spangler is a pantheist). If everything in the universe is God, he reasons, then how could there be a distinct evil angelic entity?

Spangler, like some other New Agers, believes in a single God-force that has both a *positive* pole (a force known as the Christ) and a *negative* pole (a force known as Lucifer). "Christ" and "Lucifer" are two sides of the same coin. The Christ energies and Lucifer energies work together in keeping the universe in a cosmic balance.[2] (Such an idea is not unlike "the force" in the *Star Wars* movies, which has both a light side and a dark side.)

The Christadelphians, categorized as a cult of Christianity,[3] claim Satan is not a real supernatural angelic person but refers to the human tendency to engage in sin. They believe "Satan" is an evil principle deep in human nature, inclining people to evil acts.[4]

Satanists have different views about Satan.[5] Some believe what the Bible says about Satan (and God), but they have given allegiance to Satan even though they understand they may have to suffer eternal punishment in hell after death. Others hold to a more dualistic concept, believing that both God and Satan are equal and opposite spiritual forces—either of which human beings can use to achieve their goals in life. Still others interpret Satan to be a force that governs the world of nature, and that they can harness this force to bring about their personal desires. Still others—unquestionably the majority—use the term *Satan* as a metaphorical way to symbolize their rejection of the Christian faith, which they interpret to be a powerless religion that involves nothing more than self-sacrifice, self-denial, and oppression.

Modern Wicca—prevalent today among teenagers and women who seek personal empowerment—has become popular because of such books as *Wicca: A Guide for the Solitary Practitioner* by Scott Cunningham; *The Craft: A Witch's Book of Shadows* by Dorothy Morrison; and *The Element Encyclopedia of 5000 Spells: The Ultimate Reference Book for the Magical Arts* by Judika Illes. These books express a disbelief in Satan. This may come as a surprise to some Christians, for many incorrectly believe that Wicca and Satanism are essentially the same. They are not.[6]

Many people in modern Western culture claim that *Satan* refers to a personification of evil. A personification involves the representation of an idea in the form of a person. An example is how sin in the Old Testament crouches at the door, ready to pounce on a person (Genesis 4:6-7). In similar fashion, many today believe Satan personifies all that is evil in the world.

It is regrettable that we often find caricatures of the devil in popular media today that make fun of the very idea of a personal devil. Some, for example, portray the devil as a reddish, two-horned, pointy-tailed, impish-looking creature who carries a pitchfork. The late stand-up comic Flip Wilson made a fortune causing millions of people to laugh with his famous "the devil made me do it" line. The idea communicated in all this is that belief in Satan is childish.

There is a lack of recognition of Satan and his influence even in some conservative churches. Bible-believing pastors and laypeople sometimes seem reluctant to "give the devil his due." Bible scholar Harold Willmington enlightens us on this:

> Suppose there is a Bible-believing church which is going through a spiritual crisis. For some months no soul has walked its aisles. The attendance and offerings are down and the members are becoming restless. All Bible pastors have had these experiences. Finally, in desperation, a special committee is appointed by the congregation to discover the source of this coldness and lifelessness. After considerable prayer and probing, the committee submits its report. What are its findings? I believe it may be safely assumed that the average committee would lay the blame on one or more of the following: (1) the pastor; (2) certain officials; (3) a cold congregation; or (4) a difficult neighborhood.
>
> But what fact-finding group would return the following indictment? We believe the main source of our heartaches for the past few months is satanic! We believe the reason no souls have been saved recently is due to an all-out attack on our church by the devil! We close this report with a strong recommendation that the congregation call a special meeting, rebuke Satan, plead the blood of Christ and claim the victory![7]

Willmington concludes: "If I were the devil I would deny my existence in the world and downplay it in the local church, thus freeing me to go about my business unheeded, unhindered, and unchecked."[8] This reminds me of one of my favorite Christian writers, C.S. Lewis, who wrote, "There are two equal and opposite errors into which our race can fall about the devils. One is to disbelieve in their existence. The other is to believe, and to feel an excessive and unhealthy interest in them. They themselves are equally pleased by both errors."[9]

Lewis's point is insightful!

I'm convinced Satan himself has been busy promoting nonbelief in his existence on a global scale. It is a sound strategy: If there is no real personal enemy, then there will be no preparation for defense against that personal enemy. If there is no preparation for defense, the enemy can attack at will and work his evil while remaining completely incognito.

The Biblical Evidence for Satan's Existence

There is scarcely a culture, tribe, or society in this world that does not have some concept or fear of an invisible evil power. Christian missionaries and secular anthropologists alike attest to this. Witch doctors, shrunken heads, voodoo dolls, and totem poles all give dramatic evidence of this universal fear.

What do the Christian Scriptures teach? The Bible is the Christian's barometer of truth. We test all spiritual truth claims against the Bible (Acts 17:11). In Scripture we discover the real truth about Satan and demons.

The biblical evidence for the existence and activity of Satan and demons is formidable. Seven books in the Old Testament specifically teach the reality of Satan—Genesis, 1 Chronicles, Job, Psalms, Isaiah, Ezekiel, and Zechariah (for example, Genesis 3; 1 Chronicles 21:1; Job 2:1; Zechariah 3:1-2).

Every New Testament writer—and nineteen New Testament books—also refer to Satan. *Devil,* another term for Satan, occurs thirty-five times in the New Testament (for example, Matthew 4:1; 1 Peter 5:8-9; James 4:7; 1 John 3:8; Jude 9).

Interestingly, out of twenty-nine references to Satan in the four Gospels, Jesus made twenty-five of them. Anything Jesus talks a lot about is something you and I need to pay attention to (see, for example, Matthew 4:10; 25:41; Luke 10:18; 22:31-32; John 8:44).

In view of the foregoing evidence, we conclude that a denial of Satan's existence amounts to a denial of both the statements of Scripture and the testimony of the Savior Himself.

Satan Is a Real Person

Scripture reveals that Satan is a person. When I call Satan a person, however, I do not mean that he is a human being. I mean that he is a spirit being who has all the attributes of personality—*mind, emotions,* and *will.*

We know Satan has a mind and intelligence because he uses intelligent tactics to deceive people. Paul warned the Corinthian Christians, "I am afraid that as the serpent deceived Eve by his cunning, your thoughts will be led astray from a sincere and pure devotion to Christ" (2 Corinthians 11:3). Only a person can purposefully engage in deception.

Satan also has emotions. He will become "furious" with Israel during the future tribulation period (Revelation 12:17). He abhors the racial lineage of the Messiah, Jesus Christ. He also manifests the emotions of desire (Isaiah 14:13-14), jealousy (Job 1:8-9), hate (1 Peter 5:8), and anger (Revelation 12:12).

We know Satan has a will, for he volitionally rebelled against God (Isaiah 14:12-14). He literally *willed* to take God's place.

Satan's will is also clear in that he gives commands (Luke 4:3,9) and leads a rebellion against God and His people (Revelation 20:7-9).

Other persons in both the Old and New Testaments interacted with Satan as a real person. One example is how Satan verbally interacted with God about Job (Job 1). He also dialogued with Jesus: "The tempter came and said to him, 'If you are the Son of God, command these stones to become loaves of bread'" (Matthew 4:3). Jesus met each of the devil's temptations with strategic Scripture quotations and defeated him.

We can also observe that the names, titles, and ascriptions used of Satan would make sense only if he were a person. For example, Satan is the evil one (John 17:15; 1 John 5:18-19), the accuser of our brothers (Revelation 12:10), the tempter (Matthew 4:3; 1 Thessalonians 3:5), the ruler of this world (John 12:31), the god of this world (2 Corinthians 4:4), and the prince of the power of the air (Ephesians 2:2). Satan is a real—*albeit evil*—person.

Still further, other persons in both the Old and New Testaments use personal pronouns to describe him (Job 1; Matthew 4:1-11). He also engages in a variety of personal actions (Matthew 4:1-11; John 8:44; 1 John 3:8; Jude 9).

Satan's Existence Illustrated in Job

There is perhaps no more potent example of undeserved pain and suffering than Job, an upright and godly man (Job 1:1). One minute everything was fine in Job's life; the next he had lost nearly everything—his family, his wealth, and his health (1:6–2:10).

Job had no idea of what was going on behind the scenes in "the heavenly places" (Ephesians 6:12). He did not understand that his body was serving as a spiritual battleground between God and Satan. He was blind to the reality that the powers of darkness had launched an insidious assault against him and that God purposefully allowed this assault.

You and I are fortunate. We have the book of Job to inform us about Satan's behind-the-scenes activities. Job had no such book. To him, it seemed like his calamities had perfectly natural explanations: The Sabeans took his oxen and donkeys; fire from heaven—perhaps lightning—burned his sheep; the Chaldeans took his camels; and a great wind (a tornado?) wrecked his oldest son's house and killed his children. The truth is, *Satan was behind all of this*!

When we encounter sufferings in life, it may appear that there are natural explanations for all of them, but in reality there may be a satanic or demonic attack behind them. This happened in Job's life, and it may well happen to us. The problem is that our earthly perspective has limitations, and we often cannot know whether there is spiritual warfare going on behind the scenes. I therefore suggest:

- Trust in God and depend on Him, no matter what. Our painful circumstances may or *may not* relate to a demonic attack. Let's follow Proverbs 3:5: "Trust in the LORD with all your heart, and do not lean on your own understanding."

- God is never blind about why bad things happen to us, and, in fact, He always has a good purpose for allowing whatever circumstances come our way (Romans 8:28). That is all the more reason to trust Him.

- Cover all your bases. Pray specifically that God will remedy your painful circumstance (Philippians 4:6-7). But also make sure there is no sin in your life that has given place to the devil for an attack (Ephesians 4:26-27). Be sure to keep your spiritual armor on (Ephesians 6:10-18), resist the devil (1 Peter 5:8-9), and stand strong in your position in Christ (Ephesians 1:3-14). (I'll address these victory steps later in the book.)

A second insight we glean from the book of Job is that Satan cannot freely do whatever he wishes to do. He is on a leash. God has set parameters around him beyond which he is not free to go (see Job 1:12; 2:6). If there were no such parameters, you and I would surely be dead right now because Satan hates both God and His children, and he would delight in murdering us (see John 8:44).

Despite these limiting parameters, Satan's warfare against Christians is intense. It will intensify dramatically the deeper we go into the end times.

Satan's Origin

It is understandable that many wonder where Satan came from. Satan's name in ages past was Lucifer. He was an angel of unparalleled beauty and might, and his fall changed the course of cosmic history. The cause of this fall was pride. Scripture affirms of Lucifer:

> You were blameless in your ways
>   from the day you were created,
>   till unrighteousness was found in you...
> Your heart was proud because of your beauty;
>   you corrupted your wisdom for the sake of your splendor
>   (Ezekiel 28:15,17).

Lucifer became so impressed with his own beauty, brilliance, intelligence, power, and position that he began to desire for himself the honor and glory that belonged to God alone. The sin that corrupted Lucifer was self-generated pride. This pride is illustrated in Lucifer's five "I wills" recorded in Isaiah 14:13-14.

"I will ascend to heaven." Apparently Lucifer wanted to abide in heaven and desired equal recognition alongside God Himself.

"I will set my throne on high," which is *"above the stars of God."* The stars likely have reference to the angels of God. Lucifer apparently desired to rule over the angelic realm with the same authority as God Himself.

"I will sit on the mount of assembly." Scripture elsewhere reveals that such mounts can refer to the center of God's kingdom rule (see Isaiah 2:2; Psalm 48:2). The term can even refer to the Messiah's future earthly rule in Jerusalem during the millennial kingdom. Perhaps Satan desired to rule over humans in place of the Messiah.

"I will ascend above the heights of the clouds." In the Bible, clouds often metaphorically represent the glory of God (Exodus 13:21; 40:28-34; Matthew 26:64; Revelation 14:14). Apparently Lucifer sought a glory equal to that of God Himself.

"I will make myself like the Most High." Scripture describes God as the possessor of heaven and earth (Genesis 14:18-19). Lucifer apparently sought the supreme position of the universe for himself. He wanted to exercise the authority and control over the world that rightfully belongs to God alone. His sin was a direct challenge to God's authority. God, of course, judged Satan for this sin (Ezekiel 28:17).

Satan's sin had widespread effects. It affected both the angels (Revelation 12:7) and human beings (Ephesians 2:2), and it positioned him as the ruler of this world (John 16:11). Satan's act of rebellion was one of unfathomable consequences.

The Evidence for Demons

Just as there are many proofs for the existence of Satan, so there are many proofs for the existence of demonic spirits. Foremost is that Scripture refers to demons as wicked spirit beings (Leviticus 17:7; Deuteronomy 32:17; Psalm 106:37; Matthew 4:24; 7:22; 8:16,28,31,33; 9:32-34; 10:8; 11:18; 12:22,24,27,28; 15:22; 17:15,18; Mark 1:32,34,39; 3:15). A perusal of Matthew's Gospel proves that Jesus believed in the existence of demons—and even encountered them many times.

There are other proofs. An important one relates to the consistent and relentless attacks against Israel. As my friend Norman Geisler notes, "Israel as a people, considering their relative insignificance in the history of the world, have been the continual, repeated victims of conquest and genocide."[10] This conspiracy of hatred against the Jews is best explained as emanating from Satan and demons, with their relentless opposition to God's plans for Israel, which gave birth to the divine Messiah, Jesus Christ. We can say the same about the over two millennia of relentless attacks against Christians. The universality of temptation and evil in the world, alongside the proliferation of deception in the world, lends further support for the existence of demonic spirits (see 1 Timothy 4:1-2).[11]

Scripture portrays demons as real persons. Other persons use personal pronouns for them (Luke 8:27-30). They have personal names (Luke 8:30). They engage in speech with others (Luke 4:33-35,41; 8:28-30). And they manifest intelligence (Mark 1:23-24; Luke 4:34; 8:28). They are just as real as any other persons mentioned in Scripture.

The Origin of Demons

There are several theories about the origin of demons—including the spirits of deceased people, the spirits of a pre-Adamic race, and the offspring of angels and women (see Genesis 6:2). Most Christian theologians believe that when Lucifer rebelled against God, he fell from his place of prominence and led with him a host of lower-ranking angels. This is my view. In support of it, Revelation 12:4 affirms that Satan's "tail swept down a third of the stars of heaven and cast them to the earth." The Bible sometimes uses the word *stars* for angels (see Job 38:7). If stars refer to angels in Revelation 12:4, it would appear that after Lucifer rebelled against God, he drew a third of the angelic realm after him. When he sinned, he did not sin alone but apparently led a massive angelic revolt against God. Just a few verses later, we read of "the dragon and his angels" (Revelation 12:7; see also Ephesians 3:10; 6:12). The dragon is Satan, just as the fallen angels are demons.

Ranks Among the Fallen Angels

God's holy angels have ranks. Colossians 1:16 refers to them as "thrones or dominions or rulers or authorities." All angels answer to the top-ranking archangel Michael, and angels as a company—bar none—answer to Jesus Christ (Colossians 1:16).

The fallen angels also have ranks. Ephesians 6:12 speaks of them as the rulers, the authorities, the cosmic powers over this present darkness, and the spiritual forces of evil in the heavenly places. All fallen angels answer to their commander-in-chief Satan, elsewhere called "the prince of demons" (Mark 3:22; Luke 11:15).

The Need to Understand Satanic/Demonic Tactics

Satan and his fallen angels (demons) have developed specific tactics to bring Christians down—or to put it more directly, to bring *you* down. The apostle Paul refers to Satan's "designs"—his evil schemes (2 Corinthians 2:11). *Satan has a game plan to bring ruination to your life.*

Satan is tricky in how he does it. Genesis 3:1 tells us that the serpent (Satan) is "subtle and crafty" (AMPC) or "cunning" (CSB) or "shrewd" (NET). He is a master deceiver. Paul therefore warned the Corinthian Christians, "I am afraid that as the serpent deceived Eve by his cunning, your thoughts will be led astray from a sincere and pure devotion to Christ" (2 Corinthians 11:3).

Paul—an apostle with substantial experience in dealing with the devil—understandably urges us to "stand against the schemes of the devil" (Ephesians 6:11). Or as the Amplified Bible renders it, "Stand up against all the schemes and the strategies and the deceits of the devil."

It is a given that if you desire to stand against the devil's tactics, you first need to understand what those tactics are. That is one reason I wrote this book. I intend to reveal what I consider the most likely tactics the devil will try to use to defeat you spiritually and reduce you to a powerless Christian, depressed and wallowing in pain.

But I'll also spend a great deal of time addressing the Lord's provisions for us to have victory in spiritual warfare—especially our position "in Christ." I will repeat it often: The sheep who are safest from the vicious wolves are those who stay nearest to the Shepherd.

> Father, by the power of Your Spirit, please enable us to understand the Old and New Testament verses we will consult throughout the rest of this book about Satan and demons. Please help us to first understand who the enemy is and then learn about the infernal tactics utilized by the kingdom of darkness. Most of all, help us understand Your provisions for victory in spiritual

warfare. Through it all, I ask that You instill a sense of awe in each of us for the person, the words, and the works of our Lord Jesus Christ—who Himself defeated all the powers of darkness at the cross. I thank You in His awesome name. Amen.

2

The Character and Goal of Satan and His Fallen Angels

S atan's "ultimate intention is to ruin you. Your destruction is his highest priority."[1] That's the assessment of pastor Erwin Lutzer.

Satan can attack a Christian physically (Job 2:7-8) and spiritually (Job 1:11; 2:5,9). He can sift Christians (Luke 22:31-32) and even fill their hearts to lie (Acts 5:3-4). If permitted by God, he can engage in destruction of the flesh (1 Corinthians 5:5). He can tempt Christians (1 Corinthians 7:5; 1 Thessalonians 3:5) and harass them (2 Corinthians 12:7). He seeks to hinder Christians (1 Thessalonians 2:18), ensnare them (1 Timothy 3:7; 2 Timothy 2:26), devour them (1 Peter 5:8), accuse them (Revelation 12:10), and cause them strife (Ephesians 4:25-27; 1 John 3:8-12). He will do anything he can to obstruct the purposes God desires to accomplish through Christ and His followers (Luke 22:31-32; Acts 13:10; 1 Thessalonians 2:18; Revelation 2:10; 12:13-17).

Satan is also relentless in promoting false philosophies (Colossians 2:8), false ministers (2 Corinthians 11:14-15), false doctrine

(1 Timothy 4:1; 2 Peter 2:1), false religions with false gospels (Galatians 1:6,8), and idolatry (1 Corinthians 10:19-20). If he can't injure you, he will seek to deceive you.

Meanwhile, demons are busy extending Satan's activities worldwide (Ephesians 6:11-12) and opposing the plan of God in any way possible (Daniel 10:10-14; Revelation 16:13-16). Lewis Sperry Chafer suggests that "their influence is exercised both to mislead the unsaved and to wage an unceasing warfare against the believer (Eph. 6:12)."[2]

Demons can cause both mental and physical afflictions (1 Samuel 16:14; Matthew 9:33; 12:22; 17:15-18; Mark 5:4-5; Luke 8:27-29; 9:37-42). They promote immorality and perversity (Leviticus 18:6-30; Deuteronomy 18:9-14), idolatry (Leviticus 17:7; Deuteronomy 32:17; Psalm 106:36-38; 1 Corinthians 10:20; Revelation 9:20), and false doctrines (1 Timothy 4:1; 1 John 4:4). They oppose biblical truth (1 Timothy 3:16–4:3), hinder answers to the prayers of believers (Daniel 10:12-20), and seek to incite division among believers as well as persecution against believers (James 3:13-16; Revelation 13:7). They are ceaseless in their attacks, just as Satan is.

We learn a lot about Satan's character and goals by the various names and titles used of him in Scripture. Let's consider some select examples.

The Accuser of Our Brothers

Revelation 12:10 describes Satan as the accuser of our brothers. The Greek text of this verse reveals that accusing God's people is a continuous, ongoing work of Satan. He never lets up; he accuses God's people "day and night."

Thomas Ice and Robert Dean suggest that "Satan opposes God's people in two ways. First, he brings charges against believers before God (Zechariah 3:1; Romans 8:33). Second, he accuses believers to their own conscience."[3] By so doing, he seeks to bring ruination to believers.

When Satan accuses us, it is comforting to know that we have a defense attorney. His name is Jesus Christ. In 1 John 2:1 the apostle John says, "I am writing these things to you so that you may not sin. But if anyone does sin, we have an advocate with the Father, Jesus Christ the righteous." The word *advocate* in the original Greek means "defense attorney" (see also Romans 8:34; 1 Timothy 2:5; Hebrews 7:25). Whenever Satan accuses us before God's throne, Jesus defends our case.

In my mind's eye, I can picture Satan appearing before God's throne (the Judge) and saying, "God, how can you call Ron Rhodes a Christian? Did you see what he just did? He sinned! He's as fallen a creature as they come!"

At that moment, Jesus Christ—my defense attorney—steps up to the throne and says, "Father, Ron Rhodes trusted me for salvation in 1971. I paid for all his sins at the cross of Calvary."

The Father immediately renders His verdict: "Case dismissed!"

It is important for us to remember this whenever Satan accuses us in our consciences. His accusations can make us feel like worms before God if we let them. We must stand strong on the promises of God regarding our complete forgiveness in Christ (2 Corinthians 5:21; Ephesians 1:7; 2:8-9).

I find it relevant that the key verse in the Bible on Satan as "accuser of our brothers" is in the context of the end times. Revelation 12:10 affirms: "I heard a loud voice in heaven, saying, 'Now the salvation and the power and the kingdom of our God and the authority of his Christ have come, for the accuser of our brothers has been thrown down, who accuses them day and night before our God.'" This takes place at the midpoint of the tribulation period, right after a major battle takes place between the holy angels and the fallen angels. Satan and the fallen angels will be defeated and cast from the heavenlies down to the earth in judgment (12:7-9). This will make the devil ferocious: "Woe to you, O earth and sea, for the devil has come down to you in great wrath, because he knows that his time is short!" (Revelation 12:12). Things are about to get much worse on planet Earth.

Our Adversary and "Roaring Lion"

First Peter 5:8 describes Satan as a vicious adversary: "Be sober-minded; be watchful. Your adversary the devil prowls around like a roaring lion, seeking someone to devour." Such words reveal that Satan opposes us and stands against us in every way he can. He hates us because we love Jesus. He is relentless in his opposition to us.

Notice that Peter urges us to be "sober-minded" about our adversary. This means we should be "intelligent concerning the stratagems of Satan."[4] There must be "constant vigilance, a preparedness to meet every attack of the wicked one."[5]

Peter also said we must be "watchful." This means we must remain on high alert. Satan is cunning and cruel, attacking Christians when they least expect it, just like a predatory lion moves in on helpless prey. In the same way that lions attacked and ate Christians in the Roman Coliseum during Nero's reign in the first century, so now Satan seeks to attack and chew up Christians whenever given the opportunity.

Satan's adversarial activities will explode against both Jews and Christians during the future tribulation period. The attacks he will launch against both groups will be unprecedented.

Satan's Lion-Like Attacks Against the Jews. Revelation 12:12 warns: "The devil has come down to you in great wrath, because he knows that his time is short." Verse 13 gets more specific, warning us that Satan "pursued the woman [Israel] who had given birth to the male child [Jesus Christ]." This passage graphically depicts Satan's persecution of the Jews during the tribulation period. He'll do whatever he can to destroy all the Jewish people in the last half of the tribulation. This period will therefore be the "great tribulation" (Matthew 24:21) and "a time of distress" for Israel (Jeremiah 30:7).

The devil hates Israel because Christ came from this nation. David Jeremiah suggests that Satan has always wanted to destroy Israel:

> Knowing from prophecy that the Promised One would spring from Israel, the adversary did everything he could to keep that nation from being formed. He incited Esau to attempt to kill his brother, Jacob, who would father the twelve tribes of Israel...He incited Pharaoh to murder all the Jewish baby boys in Egypt. Had either Jacob or Moses not survived, the nation of Israel would never have existed...Satan incited the wicked Haman to plot the extermination of all the Jews. But God raised up Esther "for such a time as this" to expose Haman's scheme, and the promised seed was spared (Esther 4:14)...When the prophesied Child was finally born, Satan instilled fear and hatred in King Herod, who had all the babies in Bethlehem murdered. He thought that surely the promised seed would be slain in this insidious act of infanticide (Matthew 2:16).[6]

Scripture reveals that Jesus will come again *only* when the Jewish remnant—who will become believers in the Lord Jesus—face endangerment at Armageddon at the end of the tribulation period. The Jewish leaders will cry out for deliverance from Jesus, their newfound Messiah (see Zechariah 12:10). In Satan's perverted thinking, he may reason that if he can destroy the Jews during the tribulation period, then he can prevent the second coming of Christ and save himself from defeat. However, Revelation 12:14 assures that God will providentially keep watch over *and protect* the Jewish remnant from extinction during this time.

Of great significance is the fact that Satan will energize the antichrist (2 Thessalonians 2:9; Revelation 13:2). Just as Satan is a persecutor of the Jews, so the antichrist will be a persecutor of the Jews. In fact, Satan will persecute the Jews *through* the antichrist (see Matthew 24:15-21).

Satan's Lion-Like Attacks Against Christians. The antichrist will engage in great persecution not only against the Jews but also against Christians. Revelation 13:7-10 tells us that the Satan-energized antichrist "was allowed to make war on the saints and to conquer them" (see 2 Thessalonians 2:9). A parallel passage is Daniel 7:21, which reveals that the antichrist "made war with the saints and prevailed over them." Such language reveals there will be many martyrs during the tribulation period (Revelation 6:9-11). Believers in God will rather die than submit to either Satan or Satan's puppet, the antichrist.

A Murderer

Closely connected to Satan's work as an adversary is his work as a murderer. In John 8:44 Jesus reveals that the devil was "a murderer from the beginning." The word *murderer* literally means "man killer" (see 1 John 3:12,15). Hatred is the motive that leads a person to commit murder. Satan hates both God and His children, so he has a genuine motive for murder. Ray Stedman insightfully notes that "because he is a liar and a murderer, the Devil's work is to deceive and to destroy. There you have the explanation for all that has been going on in human history throughout the whole course of the record of man...Whom the Devil cannot deceive, he tries to destroy, and whom he cannot destroy, he attempts to deceive."[7]

Satan would love to murder you and me physically, and if the Lord weren't watching out for us, we'd all already be dead. If Satan cannot murder you physically, however, *he will try to murder you emotionally*. He will seek to bring ruination to you in any way he can. He is a master at using guilt, anger, depression, discouragement, and other debilitating emotions to twist Christians all out of shape. *Christian beware!*

Satan's murderous proclivities will continue into the end times in the hands of the antichrist. He will attack and murder both Jews and Christians, and anyone else who stands in the way of his personal end-times agenda. In Revelation 6:9 we read about "the souls of those who had been slain for the word of God and for the witness they had borne." While their bodies are dead on the earth, their souls are alive and well in heaven, and they ask God: "O Sovereign Lord, holy and true, how long before you will judge and avenge our blood on those who dwell on the earth?" (verse 10). God will answer their inquiry when the trumpet judgments and bowl judgments assault the earth in the latter part of the tribulation period (Revelation 8:6–9:21; 16:2–21).

The Devil ~

Scripture often refers to Satan as the devil (Matthew 4:1), a word that means "adversary" and "slanderer." Satan was and is the adversary of Christ; he is the adversary of all who follow Christ. One of his primary activities is that he slanders God to man (Genesis 3:1-7) and slanders man (specifically Christians) to God (Job 1:9; 2:4). A slanderer is someone who utters malicious false reports that injure the reputation of another. Satan seeks to injure God's reputation to the entire world, and he seeks to injure the reputation of Christians in any way he can.

We recall how Satan slandered Job before God's throne: "Does Job fear God for no reason? Have you not put a hedge around him and his house and all that he has, on every side? You have blessed the work of his hands, and his possessions have increased in the land. But stretch out your hand and touch all that he has, and he will curse you to your face" (Job 1:9-11). God proved Satan wrong in this accusation, as revealed throughout the rest of the book of Job.

Satan's slanderous proclivities continue into the end times. We see this in how his puppet leader, the antichrist, will slander God during the tribulation period. The reason the antichrist slanders God is that Satan energizes him to do so (2 Thessalonians 2:9; Revelation 13:2).

Revelation 13:5-6 reveals that the antichrist will utter "haughty and blasphemous words." He will open his mouth "to utter blasphemies against God, blaspheming his name and his dwelling, that is, those who dwell in heaven."

The root meaning of the Greek word for *blasphemy* can range from showing a lack of reverence for God to a more extreme attitude of contempt for either God or something considered sacred (see Leviticus 24:16; Matthew 26:65; Mark 2:7). It can involve speaking evil against God (Psalm 74:18; Isaiah 52:5; Romans 2:24; Revelation 13:1,6; 16:9,11,21) or showing contempt for the true God by making claims of divinity for oneself (see Mark 14:64; John 10:33). The antichrist will engage in all these aspects of blasphemy.

Notice the specific objects of the antichrist's blasphemy in Revelation 13:6. First is God's *name* ("It opened its mouth to utter blasphemies against God, *blaspheming his name*"). In biblical times, a person's name represented everything that person was. It pointed to his or her very nature. It included the very attributes of a person. For the antichrist to blaspheme God's name means that he will blaspheme God's very identity and His nature.

The antichrist will also blaspheme God's *dwelling*, or heaven (see Hebrews 9:23-24). "Those who dwell in heaven" includes both the holy angels and the glorified saints—that is, believers caught up in the rapture and then taken to heaven prior to the tribulation period. This will be the antichrist's way of saying to God, "I disdain You and everyone who associates with You."

The devil's role as slanderer will be manifest through his puppet leader, the antichrist. The antichrist—inspired by the devil—will set himself up as the only object of worship during the tribulation period, slandering the true God in the process (2 Thessalonians 2:4).

The God of This World / The Ruler of This World

Scripture reveals that the antichrist—who will claim to be God—will one day rule the entire world: "Authority was given it over every tribe and people and language and nation" (Revelation 13:7). This is not unexpected since Satan—the one who energizes the antichrist—is "the god of this world" (2 Corinthians 4:4) and "the ruler of this world" (John 12:31; 14:30; 16:11). We may surmise that Satan fulfills his ultimate ambition as god and ruler of the world by exercising these very roles through the person he energizes—the antichrist.

The Tempter

It is not surprising to find Scripture referring to Satan as the tempter (Matthew 4:3; 1 Thessalonians 3:5). This title reveals that

Satan's purpose is to incite humans to sin against God. Henry Thiessen tells us that Satan "presents the most plausible excuses and suggests the most striking advantages for sinning."[8]

Through long observation, Satan knows your personal weaknesses. He knows my personal weaknesses. He knows where we're all vulnerable. He knows the precise circumstances that might set up a particular Christian for a fall. Here is something you can bank on: Whenever Satan sees an opportunity to set up circumstances that stand a good chance of inciting you to sin, he will follow through with an attack. He is a master at it.

Satan's role as tempter will continue into the tribulation period, and the temptations will become ever stronger and ever more insidious. Allow me to give you one good example.

Scripture reveals that the false prophet—the antichrist's right-hand man—will cause "all, both small and great, both rich and poor, both free and slave, to be marked on the right hand or the forehead, so that no one can buy or sell unless he has the mark, that is, the name of the beast or the number of its name" (Revelation 13:16-17). Notice how the work of the tempter lies at the very heart of the mark of the beast. This mark will be a commerce passport during the second half of the tribulation period. It will show that one is religiously orthodox as defined by the antichrist and the false prophet. The mark will identify the submissive followers of the beast and worshipers of his image.

The critical factor is that *only* those with the mark of the beast can purchase food for themselves and their families. The temptation is powerful. I can imagine people reasoning, "I must either receive the mark of the antichrist, thus ensuring that I and my family can eat. Or I must refuse the mark of the antichrist, and we may all starve to death." All the while, Satan works behind the scenes blinding their minds to their true spiritual endangerment and their dire need for God and the true gospel (2 Corinthians 4:4).

Receiving the mark of the beast is a serious business, for Revelation 14:9-11 affirms that those who do so will be on the receiving end of God's wrath. Even before they die, they will suffer painful sores (Revelation 16:2). Any who express loyalty to the antichrist and his cause will suffer the wrath of our holy and just God (see Psalm 75:8; Isaiah 51:17; Jeremiah 25:15-16).

Christians will refuse to receive the mark of the antichrist (Revelation 20:4). I can imagine them reasoning, "If I receive the mark of the antichrist, I and my family can eat, but this act will be sinful and rebellious against the Lord. I know we must reject the mark of the antichrist. My family and I may well starve, but we know that upon death, all of us as Christians will be with the Lord, and we will live with Him eternally." It is this reasoning that will enable them to resist the tempter. They will gladly die in view of their glorious future in the afterlife.

Beelzebul

Matthew 12:24 refers to Satan as "Beelzebul, the prince of demons." Many Christian scholars believe that Beelzebul was a name for the ancient Canaanite deity Baal. Baal worship involved deviant sexual practices. Satan was obviously behind Baal worship, just as he is behind the immorality in all false religions and cults. It is thus understandable that *Beelzebul* eventually became an alternate name for Satan.

Beelzebul literally means "lord of the flies." It carries the idea "lord of filth." The devil corrupts everything he touches. Much of the moral filth in the world today results from his devious efforts. For example, we witness the lord of filth at work in the various forms of immorality in the cults. In the 1960s the Children of God cult promoted sex, nudity, and fornication among its members. In the Unification Church, the late Reverend Moon engaged in ritual sexual purification practices among female members. Among Wiccans (witches), sex is engaged in as a sacrament. A well-known feature of historic Mormonism is polygamy. There are many similar examples.

Satan as Beelzebul will continue promoting immorality in the tribulation period. The book of Revelation tells us that New Babylon, like its ancient counterpart, will feature paganism, false religion, immorality, and a strong anti-god sentiment. Revelation 17:2-3 speaks of the false one-world religion of the tribulation period—a religion emanating from New Babylon—as a great prostitute "with whom the kings of the earth have committed sexual immorality, and with the wine of whose sexual immorality the dwellers on earth have become drunk." Just as wine can have a controlling influence over people, so will this false religion have a controlling influence on the world's population. This false religious system will probably be permissive and tolerant, opening the door for people around the world to engage in any kind of immoral lifestyle they want.

The times may change, but Beelzebul continues to spew forth moral filth throughout every age!

The Father of Lies

John 8:44 refers to Satan as the "father of lies." The word *father* metaphorically refers to the originator of a family or company of persons animated by a deceitful character. Satan was the first and greatest liar. Later in the book I'll address how Satan seeks to injure you personally by his lies and deception. For now, however, allow me to narrow my attention to the end times.

Scripture reveals that there will be broad and penetrating deception in the end times. First Timothy 4:1 warns that "the Spirit expressly says that in later times some will depart from the faith by devoting themselves to deceitful spirits and teachings of demons." Second Timothy 4:3-4 likewise warns that "the time is coming when people will not endure sound teaching, but having itching ears they will accumulate for themselves teachers to suit their own passions, and will turn away from listening to the truth and wander off into myths." Satan, the father of lies, will be behind it all.

A key verse pertaining to end-times deception is 2 Thessalonians 2:3, which speaks of the coming day of the Lord. The English Standard Version renders the verse this way: "Let no one deceive you in any way. For that day will not come, unless *the rebellion* comes first, and the man of lawlessness is revealed, the son of destruction" (italics added). The New American Standard Version renders the critical part of this verse, "Let no one in any way deceive you, for it will not come unless *the apostasy* comes first" (italics added). The King James Version puts it this way: "Let no man deceive you by any means: for that day shall not come, except there come *a falling away* first" (italics added). These various translations provide insight into the apostle Paul's intended meaning. The end times will bring a "rebellion" against the truth, a great "apostasy," a "falling away" from God's truth (see also 1 Timothy 4:1-3; 2 Timothy 3:1-5; 4:3-4; James 5:1-8; 2 Peter 2; 3:3-6). Apparently, this rebellious apostasy will prepare the way for the emergence of the antichrist whom Satan will empower (John 8:44; 2 Thessalonians 2:9).

Satan, the father of lies, is the arch-deceiver of all humanity. He has long sought to bring about the ruination of humankind through deception. He does this in multifaceted ways. For example:

- He distorts the Scriptures (Genesis 3:4-5; Matthew 4:6).

- He schemes to outwit humans (2 Corinthians 2:11).

- He masks himself by appearing to others as an angel of light (2 Corinthians 11:14).

In the book of Revelation, we read that Satan deceives the nations (20:3,8). In fact, he is "the deceiver of the whole world" (Revelation 12:9). The antichrist—empowered by Satan—also deceives those on earth during the tribulation period: "The coming of the lawless one is by the activity of Satan with all power and false signs and wonders, and with all wicked deception for those who are perishing, because they refused to love the truth and so be saved" (2 Thessalonians 2:9-10). The false prophet—the antichrist's first lieutenant, who is also no doubt empowered by Satan—"deceives those who dwell on earth" (Revelation 13:14). The entire satanic trinity—Satan, the antichrist, and the false prophet—will engage in massive deception during the tribulation period.

Satan Is "the Ape of God"

Augustine referred to the devil as *Simius Dei*—"the ape of God." By this he meant that Satan is a great counterfeiter.[9] As one theologian put it, "the principal tactic Satan uses to attack God and His program in general is to offer a counterfeit kingdom and program."[10] Second Corinthians 11:14 hints at this in referring to Satan masquerading as "an angel of light."

Satan "apes" God in many ways. For example, he has…

- his own church—the "synagogue of Satan" (Revelation 2:9)

- his own ministers—ministers of darkness who bring false sermons (2 Corinthians 11:4-5)

- his own system of theology—called "teachings of demons" (1 Timothy 4:1; Revelation 2:24)

- his own ministers who proclaim a false gospel—"a gospel contrary to the one we preached to you" (Galatians 1:8)

- his own throne (Revelation 13:2) and his own worshipers (13:4)

- his own false Christs (Matthew 24:4-5)

- his own false teachers who bring in "destructive heresies" (2 Peter 2:1)

- his own false prophets (Matthew 24:11)

- his own false apostles who imitate the true (2 Corinthians 11:13)

The backdrop to Satan's counterfeit kingdom is his fall. According to Isaiah 14:13-14, Lucifer said in his heart, "I will ascend to heaven; above the stars of God I will set my throne on high…I will make myself like the Most High." Lucifer sought the supreme position of the universe for himself. He wanted to be as powerful as God. He wanted to exercise the authority and control that rightfully belongs to God alone.

God did not permit this, and He judged Lucifer, casting him down to the earth (Ezekiel 28:17). He became corrupt, and his name changed from Lucifer ("morning star") to Satan ("adversary"). Since he cannot rule over God's kingdom, he now seeks to set up his own counterfeit kingdom that stands in opposition to God's kingdom. That's why he does so much mimicking. And this mimicking will reach its climax during the tribulation period when Satan motivates the antichrist to claim deity and demand worship on a global scale.

Satan's Vast Experience

Satan has been observing human beings on earth ever since Adam and Eve were created. That means Satan has vast experience in knowing how to bring Christians down. Charles Ryrie puts it this way:

> By his very longevity Satan has acquired a breadth and depth of experience which he matches against the limited knowledge of man. He has observed other believers in every conceivable situation, thus enabling him to predict with accuracy how we will respond to circumstances. Although Satan is not omniscient, his wide experience and observation of man throughout his entire history on earth give him knowledge which is far superior to anything any man could have.[11]

This has startling implications for you and me. Satan knows precisely what tactics will most likely be successful in his attempt to turn our lives upside-down. He is a master at it. He's had many centuries of practice. *Christian beware—you are being stalked and observed as a prelude to an attack.*

Now that we understand the character and goal of Satan and the fallen angels, we will narrow our attention in the next chapter to the nature of spiritual warfare.

3

Understanding
Spiritual Warfare

N ew Christians sometimes think that because Christ is now on
their side, life will be easy from here on out. What they don't
realize is that they also have Satan's target on their back. The Christian life is more of a battleground than a playground.

The apostle Paul thus urged young Timothy to "wage the good
warfare" (1 Timothy 1:18). He instructed him to "fight the good
fight of the faith" (6:12) and to be a "good soldier of Christ Jesus"
(2 Timothy 2:3). Later, near the time of his death, Paul informed
Timothy: "I have fought the good fight, I have finished the race, I
have kept the faith" (2 Timothy 4:7).

There's no easy way around it: *Spiritual warfare is part of the normal Christian life.* As Christian scholar Clinton Arnold put it, "To
think that a Christian could avoid spiritual warfare is like imagining that a gardener could avoid dealing with weeds."[1]

Spiritual warfare involves a cosmic conflict that is waged behind the scenes in the spiritual world but has real consequences in the physical world. Even though we can't see Satan and fallen angels with our eyes, these spirit beings can do real damage to our physical well-being, our emotional well-being, and our spiritual well-being.

There's an Invisible World All Around Us

In chapter 1, I addressed how calm the prophet Elisha was in the face of being surrounded by countless enemy combatants. His servant, however, was a basket case, fearful for his life (2 Kings 6:8-23). Elisha urged, "Do not be afraid, for those who are with us are more than those who are with them" (verse 16). Elisha then asked God to open the servant's eyes, and when God did so, the servant beheld glorious warrior angels surrounding them on every side, protecting them against the enemy (verse 17).

The prophet Daniel was aware of the invisible world of spirits around him. Daniel 10:13 reveals that an angel sent by God to take care of Daniel's prayer request met resistance mid-route by a more powerful fallen angel. Only when the archangel Michael arrived to help the lesser angel was the demonic attack repelled and the lesser angel freed to carry out his task. You never know what's going on behind the scenes in the invisible spiritual world.

The apostle Paul understandably warns us: "We do not wrestle against flesh and blood, but against the rulers, against the authorities, against the cosmic powers over this present darkness, against the spiritual forces of evil in the heavenly places" (Ephesians 6:12). My friends, do not make the mistake of assuming that because you don't see an enemy with your eyes, the enemy must not exist.

The late Billy Graham has some great insights on the inability of human beings to perceive the invisible spiritual world:

While angels may become visible by choice, our eyes are not constructed to see them ordinarily any more than we can see the dimensions of a nuclear field, the structure of atoms, or the electricity that flows through copper wiring. Our ability to sense reality is limited: The deer of the forest far surpass our human capacity in their keenness of smell. Bats possess a phenomenally sensitive built-in radar system. Some animals can see things in the dark that escape our attention. Swallows and geese possess sophisticated guidance systems that appear to border on the supernatural. So why should we think it strange if men fail to perceive the evidences of angelic presence?[2]

The invisible world of angels is all around us. You and I are typically unaware of it, but a spiritual world is there. God's holy angels, Satan, and a host of demonic spirits dwell there. That means your enemy is invisible, *but he is real*!

Key Elements of the War

Six clear factors emerge when we examine the various Scripture verses that touch on spiritual warfare:

1. There is, in fact, a spiritual war raging all around us (2 Corinthians 10:3-5).

2. We have an enemy. Paul described the spiritual enemy as the rulers, the authorities, the cosmic powers over this present darkness, and the spiritual forces of evil in the heavenly places (Ephesians 6:12). This enemy force seeks to deceive and destroy us. If it can't destroy us, it will seek to discourage, demoralize, and dishearten us, sowing seeds of doubt in our hearts.

3. It is not enough to know an enemy exists. We must learn about Satan and the fallen angels and understand their tactics. Kay Arthur is correct when she says, "The first rule of battle is this: *know your enemy*. A thorough knowledge of the opponent's strength, his probable line of attack, and his tactics are vital to achieving victory."[3]

4. We should respect our enemy but not fear him. We must become aware of Satan's methods but not become preoccupied with them. Because Satan is limited in power and God is all-powerful, we need not fear him if we follow God's instructions on spiritual warfare.

5. You are a targeted person. There's a big bull's-eye right on your back. "Satan is locked and loaded, and his bullets have our names on them. If we don't want to end up on the casualty list, we have to understand this battle and arm ourselves with God's powerful resources. The enemy has us in his crosshairs."[4]

6. You are a soldier. J.C. Ryle tells us: "The true Christian is called to be a soldier and must behave as such from the day of his conversion to the day of his death. He is not meant to live a life of religious ease, indolence, and security. He must never imagine for a moment that he can sleep and doze along the way to heaven."[5]

Spiritual Believers at Highest Risk

Not every Christian is at equal risk of being targeted by Satan. Only Christians who seek to live for Christ—who seek to live in obedience to Him and shine as lights in a dark world—are at highest risk from the powers of darkness. The more spiritual and victorious the believer, the greater the satanic and demonic assaults against him.

Chip Ingram identifies five circumstances that might cause an escalation of spiritual warfare in your life:

1. Spiritual warfare will escalate if you take significant steps toward spiritual growth.

2. Spiritual warfare will escalate if you invade enemy territory, such as engaging in evangelism or going on a mission trip.

3. Spiritual warfare will escalate if you seek to expose Satan and his tactics—like this book does. (Thank You, Jesus, for Your protection.)

4. Spiritual warfare will escalate if you repent of long-held sins and make a clean break with the world system so you can live more vibrantly for Christ.

5. Spiritual warfare will escalate if God is preparing you for a great work for His glory.[6]

Ingram's points are well taken. Anything that increases the commitment of a believer, involves reaching the lost, or brings great glory to God will be met with significant spiritual resistance.

Avoiding Extremes

The common view of liberal Christians is that Satan and demons do not exist. They view wicked spirits as a part of the mythical world prevalent in ancient times. Others today look for demons in just about everything bad that occurs. If the computer freezes up, it must be a demon. If someone sneezes, it must be a demon. This excessive view of demons is as spiritually unhealthy as it is unbiblical.

Here's a tidbit of advice based on what I've learned through the years: The single best way to maintain a balanced understanding of spiritual warfare is to base 100 percent of your understanding on Scripture alone. I urge you to be like the Bereans, who made a habit of "examining the Scriptures daily to see if these things were so" (Acts 17:11). And as 1 Thessalonians 5:21 puts it, "test everything;

hold fast what is good." The Scriptures will keep you balanced and on the right track.

Satan's Allies

Scripture reveals that Satan has two powerful allies in accomplishing his dastardly deeds among human beings: the world and the flesh. Just as allies play a critical role in any war scenario, so the world and the flesh play a critical role in Satan's goal of overcoming Christians.

Ally 1: The World. The word *world,* when used in Scripture, often refers not to the physical planet (Earth) but to an anti-God system headed by Satan. First John 5:19 tells us that "the whole world lies in the power of the evil one," who is Satan. Before we were Christians, you and I followed the ways of the world without hesitation (Ephesians 2:2). But when we became Christians, we got a new master—Jesus Christ—who calls us to be separate from the world. Scripture portrays the world as a seducer. It perpetually seeks to distract our attention and devotion away from God. First John 2:15-17 warns us:

> Do not love the world or the things in the world. If anyone loves the world, the love of the Father is not in him. For all that is in the world—the desires of the flesh and the desires of the eyes and pride of life—is not from the Father but is from the world. And the world is passing away along with its desires, but whoever does the will of God abides forever.

The apostle Paul also urges us: "Do not be conformed to this world, but be transformed by the renewal of your mind" (Romans 12:2). We are to "renounce ungodliness and worldly passions" (Titus 2:12). We must keep ourselves "unstained from the world" (James

1:27). This is important, for "friendship with the world is enmity with God" (James 4:4).

There are many things in the world that appeal to our sin nature. If we give in to these things, they inevitably drive our affections away from God. There is no neutral ground. Worldly entrapments include money, material possessions, fame, a career, entertainment, pleasure, and many other things. None of these is wrong or evil in themselves. But used wrongly, they have the potential to shift our attention away from Christ as our top priority. Any of these can sidetrack us into the web of worldliness.

Ally 2: The Flesh. Another subtle enemy of the Christian—and ally of Satan—is the flesh. The Bible uses the term *flesh* to describe that force within each of us that is in total rebellion against God. This "sin nature" was not a part of man when God created him. Rather, it entered Adam and Eve the moment they disobeyed God. Since the time of Adam and Eve, all human beings have been born into the world with a "flesh nature" or "sin nature" that rebels against God. As one Bible scholar put it, "The flesh is the inner propensity or inclination to do evil. It is the part of our creatureliness tainted by the fall that remains with us until the day we die. It is our continuing connection to this present evil age."[7]

Manifestations of the flesh include hatred, discord, jealousy, fits of rage, selfish ambition, dissensions, factions, envy, and drunkenness (Galatians 5:20-21). These kinds of things hinder our relationship with God.

Keep in mind that when you and I became Christians, the flesh or sin nature remained in us. It stays with us until we die or get raptured, whichever comes first. Until that day, the flesh will be ever present. The late J. Dwight Pentecost notes how the devil and the flesh work together: "We all live in an unredeemed body in the midst of an unredeemed creation, with an unredeemed nature within us. We have an enemy without who constantly oppresses us, and an enemy within that is ever present with us."[8]

These three—the world, the flesh, and the devil—typically work in concert with each other. They combine their efforts as a deadly trio. If we confronted each of them one at a time—with some of our conflicts with Satan alone, some with the world alone, and some with the flesh alone—then maybe things would be a little easier. But these three work together to bring about our ruination. It's a gang attack. That's what we face daily.

Giving Opportunity to the Devil

Ephesians 4:26-27 instruct us: "Be angry and do not sin; do not let the sun go down on your anger, and give no opportunity to the devil" (compare with 2 Corinthians 10:4). If there's one thing this verse tells us, it's that a Christian can, in fact, give "opportunity" to the devil to work in his or her life. In context, sinful anger in a Christian gives an opportunity to the devil. But Christian leaders agree that *any* unconfessed or persistent sin can give an opportunity to the devil and demonic spirits. This means that if you want to have victory in spiritual warfare, you must deal with unrepentant sin.

Satan is always watching for an opportunity to bring us down. He knew Job's strengths (Job 1:6-12; 2:1-7) and Peter's weaknesses (Luke 22:31). He knows our weaknesses too, and he is always probing for an opening in our lives. Demons are "eager to gain some kind of access to our lives so they can make us as miserable and unproductive as possible."[9] Unrepentant and unconfessed sin make such access easy.

The late Warren Wiersbe warns that "if the believer cultivates in his life any known sin, he is giving Satan an opportunity to get a foothold, a beachhead in his life. Satan will then use this opportunity to invade and take over other areas." That is why we must take a guarded approach and deal with all known sin in our lives. Wiersbe says "the area in our life that we leave unguarded is sure to be the very place that Satan attacks."[10]

The wisest policy is an immediate confession of our sin to God as soon as the sin surfaces. That quickly restores our sense of fellowship with God (1 John 1:9) *and* removes opportunity from the devil (Ephesians 4:27).

The Greek word for *confess* literally means "to say the same thing." So, when we confess our sin to God, that means we're saying the same thing about our sin that God says about it. We're agreeing with God that we engaged in a wrongdoing. No excuses!

Following my confession, I can thank God for His forgiveness based on Jesus' death on the cross on my behalf. This instantly restores my fellowship with the Father. My goal from that point forward is to walk in the power of the Holy Spirit so I'll have the power to resist committing the sin again (Galatians 5:16).

Here's an analogy: Sometimes we can develop an open sore on our body. So long as we deal with it quickly by disinfecting it and covering it, the sore will heal up and all will be well. But if we do not deal with it, the infection gets worse and it will hurt more. The single wisest thing we can do when we get such a sore is to take immediate steps to treat it.

Likewise, if a Christian gives opportunity to the devil through sin, the single wisest thing he or she can do is to confess that sin immediately so that instead of allowing the devil to continue making things worse, spiritual healing comes through confession.

Don't make the mistake of engaging in partial obedience to the Lord. And don't rationalize or make excuses for your sin. Such halfhearted commitment will not remove opportunity from the devil. Confess your sin with a sincere, repentant heart.

Christians: Possession, Oppression, or Demonized?

Some Christians believe Christians can be demon possessed. Others say they can only be oppressed or influenced by demons. Still others say they can be "demonized." There are lots of opinions on the matter.

Demon possession may be defined as…

> a demon residing in a person, exerting direct control and influence over that person, with certain derangement of mind and/or body. Demon possession is to be distinguished from demon influence or demon activity in relation to a person. The work of the demon in the latter is from the outside; in demon possession it is from within.[11]

A person who is demon possessed may manifest unusual, superhuman strength (Mark 5:2-4). He may act in bizarre ways, such as going nude and living among tombs rather than in a house (Luke 8:27). The possessed person often engages in self-destructive behavior (Matthew 17:15; Mark 5:5). These are just a few of the biblical signs of demon possession.

According to the definition given above, demons cannot possess Christians because the Holy Spirit perpetually indwells them (1 Corinthians 6:19). I like the way my old friend Walter Martin used to put it. He said that when the devil comes knocking on the door of the Christian's heart, the Holy Spirit opens it and says, "Get lost!"

Not once does Scripture record a Christian being demon possessed. To clarify, there are examples of Christians being afflicted by the devil, strongly influenced by the devil, and tempted by the devil, but not *possessed* by the devil *from within.*

Colossians 1:13 affirms that God "has delivered us from the domain of darkness and transferred us to the kingdom of his beloved Son." Further, "he who is in you [the Holy Spirit] is greater than he who is in the world [the devil]" (1 John 4:4). These verses would not make much sense if demons could possess a Christian from within.

Having said all this, external demonic affliction can be severe in a Christian. Charles Ryrie suggests that the demonic affliction a Christian might suffer can be so severe that it might even mimic possession:

> It is probably a good idea to make a distinction between demon possession and demon activity or influence, though it may be little more than an academic distinction. If there is a distinction, then in demon possession the base of the demon's operations is within the person possessed, while demon influence is from outside the person's being. However, the symptoms or characteristics may very well be the same whether the demon is operating from within or without. Yet if you ask whether a Christian can be demon possessed, seemingly the answer should be no, simply because the indwelling of the Holy Spirit would seem to forbid a rival power like a demon from also possessing him at the same time. But if you ask whether a Christian can be affected seriously by a demon, the answer is certainly yes; the effect of such demon activity may be the same as characterizes demon possession.[12]

Theologians largely agree that the severity of demonic affliction in a Christian often relates to unrepentant, unconfessed sin. A worldly and carnal Christian who is living in perpetual sin will experience far greater demonic bondage than a Christian who repents of and then confesses his or her sin. *Demons are ready to take as much ground as Christians will give them*!

Closing Insights on the End Times

I draw this chapter to a close with five observations about how the contents of this chapter relate to the end times:

1. *We are to "wage the good warfare" (1 Timothy 1:18), to "fight the good fight of the faith" (6:12), and to be a "good soldier of Christ Jesus" (2 Timothy 2:3).* It is a given that it will be much harder to fight the good fight during the future tribulation period when the antichrist—empowered by Satan—will reign supreme, and demonic activity will be greatly escalated.

2. *One reason it will be more difficult to fight the good fight during the tribulation period is that the church will have already been raptured.* There will be far fewer believers on the earth. Just as there is strength in numbers, so there is weakness when numbers are lacking. Gloriously, however, there will be many conversions to Christ during this period, despite heavy satanic and demonic resistance (see Revelation 7:9-17).

3. *There is an invisible world all around us, inhabited by God's holy angels, Satan, and a host of demonic spirits. This invisible world will be highly active during the tribulation period.* For example, when the antichrist engages in harsh persecution against Jews and Christians, people on earth will be unaware that he is being energized for this by the invisible devil (2 Thessalonians 2:9; Revelation 13:2). Likewise, when God's invisible angels inflict the seven trumpet judgments (Revelation 8:7–9:21) and then the seven bowl judgments

(Revelation 16:2-21), people on earth will be unaware that those angelic activities are causing such widespread destruction on planet Earth.

4. *Only Christians who seek to live for Christ are at the highest risk from the powers of darkness.* This will be all the truer during the future tribulation period, where persecution and martyrdom of Christians will be commonplace. To live for Christ may involve the death penalty for many (see Revelation 6:9-11)!

5. *One of Satan's allies in bringing Christians down is "the world."* First John 5:19 tells us that the whole world lies in the power of the devil. During the tribulation period, the devil will energize the antichrist as he assumes control of the entire world (2 Thessalonians 2:9; Revelation 13:3). This will make things all the harder for Christians.

PART 2

UNDERSTANDING ENEMY TACTICS

We are not ignorant of his designs.

(2 CORINTHIANS 2:11)

4

SATAN'S SCHEMES:

Flaming Darts, Mind Games, Guilt, and Discouragement

The apostle Paul instructs Christians to "stand against the schemes of the devil" (Ephesians 6:11). The word *schemes* is rich in the original Greek. The Amplified Bible translates it "the schemes and the strategies and the deceits of the devil." The Expanded Bible has it "the devil's evil tricks." The J.B. Phillips New Testament has it "the devil's methods of attack."

My friends, the devil has developed specific tactics characterized by deceit and trickery to bring you down and ruin you spiritually, emotionally, and even physically. He's a master at it. He's had thousands of years of experience, and he knows just which scheme will have the highest potential of injuring you. He and his fallen angels are stalking you, watching for weaknesses, probing for vulnerabilities. You are being profiled, and based on that profile the powers of darkness are designing a custom blueprint for your fall. *Christian beware!*

Flinging Flaming Darts

Every one of us as Christians are targets of "the flaming darts of the evil one" (Ephesians 6:16). There are all kinds of flaming darts the devil may fling. You might find yourself targeted with a dart of discouragement. Sometimes you might suffer a dart of doubting your faith in God or doubting your faith in the Bible or doubting your salvation. Sometimes you might experience the dart of personal offense that causes resentment in your heart toward someone. You might also suffer a dart of jealousy or covetousness or constant worry or debilitating guilt over something you've done. Perhaps you may experience a dart of lust.

Ancient warriors used flaming darts to disable and incapacitate an enemy combatant.[1] That is exactly what the devil wants to do to you. He seeks to disable and incapacitate you—through whatever dart may work—so you're no longer excited and joyful in your relationship with the Lord. I think David Jeremiah is correct in saying, "The devil has a quiver full of darts, and he sends exactly the right ones our way when we least expect it."[2]

Satan saves the deadliest darts in his quiver for Christians who seek a close and vibrant relationship with Jesus. If you have a fervent desire to serve Christ, you're a special candidate for Satan's flaming darts.

Wearing Down Your Defenses

Satan is relentless. He never gives up. If one tactic doesn't work against you, he'll quickly try another. We witness this in the devil's attempted temptations of Christ:

Then Jesus was led up by the Spirit into the wilderness to be tempted by the devil. And after fasting forty days and forty nights, he was hungry. And the tempter came and said to him, "If you are the Son of God, command these stones to become loaves of bread." But he answered, "It is written,

"'Man shall not live by bread alone,
    but by every word that comes from the mouth of God.'"

Then the devil took him to the holy city and set him on the pinnacle of the temple and said to him, "If you are the Son of God, throw yourself down, for it is written,

"'He will command his angels concerning you,' and
"'On their hands they will bear you up,
    lest you strike your foot against a stone.'"

Jesus said to him, "Again it is written, 'You shall not put the Lord your God to the test.'" Again, the devil took him to a very high mountain and showed him all the kingdoms of the world and their glory. And he said to him, "All these I will give you, if you will fall down and worship me." Then Jesus said to him, "Be gone, Satan! For it is written,

"'You shall worship the Lord your God
    and him only shall you serve.'"

Then the devil left him, and behold, angels came and were ministering to him (Matthew 4:1-11).

When one of the devil's temptations of Christ failed, he tried another. And then another. Satan does the same thing with you and me. If one of his temptations or tactics against us fails, he'll launch another, and then another. By so doing, Satan seeks to wear down our defenses so we end up defeated. He will patiently keep coming after us. We must be just as persistent in resisting him (James 4:7; 1 Peter 5:7-9).

Messing with Your Mind

Christian leaders differ over whether Satan and demons can influence our thoughts. Among those persuaded against this possibility is Mark Hitchcock, who writes:

> In Job 1–2, Satan is turned loose on Job to attack him on every front, short of taking his life. However, there is no mention of Satan planting thoughts or desires in Job's mind. His assaults are all external. This is an argument from silence, but if Satan had the power to plant thoughts in people's minds, surely he would have unleashed this attack on Job as part of the all-out assault allowed by God. The fact that he did not plant thoughts in Job's mind indicates to me that he does not have the prerogative to do so.[3]

This is a persuasive argument even if it is from silence. Other Christian leaders have a different viewpoint. Billy Graham writes: "At times, the devil apparently does put evil thoughts in our head, or even directly incites us to do evil. I think of Judas, for example, who made a secret arrangement to betray Jesus to His enemies. When Judas went to inform them where they could find Jesus, the Bible says that 'Satan entered into him' (John 13:27)." Graham suggests that "the farther we are from God, the more vulnerable we will be to Satan's attacks." Graham cautions, "Not all evil thoughts come directly from Satan, however. Often they come from within—from our own sinful hearts."[4]

Some Christian leaders who believe Satan can influence our

thoughts are careful to qualify that Satan cannot speak *from within* the Christian's mind, but only external to the believer. After all, Christians cannot be demon possessed. One Christian leader put it this way:

> If we open the door to Satan by failing to put on the full armor of God, he does, as it were, sit on our shoulders and whisper into our ears. The whisper cannot be discerned with the physical ear; it can, however, penetrate "the ear" of the mind. We cannot explain how such communication takes place any more than we can explain how our immaterial minds can cause the physical synapses of the brain to fire. But that such mind-to-mind communication takes place is indisputable. If it were not so, the devil could not have tempted Judas to betray his Master, seduced Ananias and Sapphira to deceive Peter, or incited David to take a census.[5]

Judas made a volitional choice *in his mind* to engage in a betrayal of Christ. He made a *mental choice* to commit this sinful act. The devil apparently influenced his mind to do this (Luke 22:3).

Ananias and Sapphira made a volitional choice *in their minds* to engage in deception to Peter and lie to the Holy Spirit. They made a *mental choice* to commit this sinful act. They did it after Satan influenced their hearts (Acts 5:3). Notice that Peter said, "*Why is it* that you have contrived this deed in your heart?" (Acts 5:4, emphasis added). Some Bible expositors suggest Peter asked why because some previous sin must have opened the door for Satan to influence Ananias's thoughts on this matter. That previous sin was likely greed and pride.

David sinfully took a census of his fighting men in Israel. He apparently did so out of pride—that is, he wanted to see how powerful he and his army were. It was apparently Satan who introduced this sinful thought into David's mind: "Satan…incited David to number Israel" (1 Chronicles 21:1). After Satan "incited" him, David made the *mental choice* to number Israel. The devil somehow influenced David's thinking.

I am persuaded that Satan somehow influenced the thought processes of Judas, Ananias and Sapphira, and David. This possibility seems to be supported by 2 Corinthians 11:3, where the apostle Paul warned the Corinthian Christians: "I am afraid that as *the serpent deceived Eve* by his cunning, *your thoughts will be led astray* from a sincere and pure devotion to Christ." Apparently, the serpent (Satan) can lead our thoughts astray. Our only defense is to fight back by filling our minds with God's truth (Romans 12:2; Ephesians 4:17-24; Philippians 4:8).

I am also persuaded that Satan is capable of influencing human thoughts in view of Paul's concern for the Thessalonian Christians, who were suffering tremendous persecution for their faith: "For this reason, when I could bear it no longer, I sent to learn about your faith, for fear that somehow the tempter had tempted you and our labor would be in vain" (1 Thessalonians 3:5). Paul's anxiety was that the Thessalonian Christians, under heavy fire for their faith, might succumb to a temptation from Satan, perhaps something similar to this: "Life will be easier for you if you drop all this Christian nonsense. Return to your pagan roots and live the good life." More to the point, Paul's concern was that—due to Satan's influence—the Thessalonians would *think wrongly* about their hard circumstances, and then *act wrongly* by abandoning their commitment.

Kay Arthur is discerning when she says that Satan's "primary tactic is to target our minds. Why? Because our thoughts determine our actions."[6] This is no doubt one reason the apostle Paul admonishes us: "We destroy arguments and every lofty opinion raised against the knowledge of God, and take every thought captive to obey Christ" (2 Corinthians 10:5). This is not a one-time event. It is a continual process. Every moment of every day, we must keep our thoughts on the right track, in submission to God, in resistance to the devil. It is not enough to resist *wrong* thinking (or *Satan-inspired* thinking); we must also pursue *right* thinking (or *God-inspired* thinking).

Having said all this, I want to add an important qualification in the interest of biblical balance. James 1:14 tells us, "Each person is tempted when he is lured and enticed by his own desire." Clearly, some of our wicked thoughts come from our own fallen flesh. But we must not interpret James 1:14 to the exclusion of the other Bible passages we have discussed.

Earlier in the book I noted that all Christians face a "gang attack" from *the world, the flesh*, and *the devil*. These three often work in concert to influence our thoughts against God. Our fallen flesh gives rise to many temptations (we have a bent toward making evil decisions). The world—the anti-God system over which the devil rules—offers many enticing allurements that can fan the temptations of the flesh into a flame. And the devil is the tempter, which means he can influence us or tempt us toward sin. We must therefore be very discerning about our thought lives.

To give you a practical example, consider what one Christian writer says about the kinds of thought attacks that might come at different times to a Christian from Satan:

> You are fat. You are ugly. No one likes you. Your prayers bounce off the ceiling, why do you bother praying anyway? You are a sexual pervert. You have committed the unforgivable sin. Read your Bible later; you are too

sleepy to read right now. Why do you bother reading your Bible? You never get anything out of it anyway because you are not a true Christian. The Bible is not true. You are stupid. You are a hypocrite.[7]

Another Bible scholar suggests the following thought attacks (described in the first person):

I'm so stupid. No one will ever love me. People would be better off if I were dead. I'm ugly. I don't deserve to be happy. There's no use trying. I'll never amount to anything. God can't love me. It's always my fault. I'm not good at anything.

I'm useless. I'm weak, no good. God must hate me. I hate myself. I might as well kill myself. I'm a bad person. Nobody cares. Why should anyone care? I'll never change. It will never get better. I'm going to die alone. Nothing I do is important. I have never done anything worthwhile. I deserve to be miserable.[8]

Such thoughts are nothing but flaming darts from the wicked one. By such darts, the devil hopes to disable and incapacitate Christians. We must not only resist such negative thoughts, we must also replace them with God's positive truth. For example: "Whatever is true, whatever is honorable, whatever is just, whatever is pure, whatever is lovely, whatever is commendable, if there is any excellence, if there is anything worthy of praise, think about these things" (Philippians 4:8). Paul urges us, "Do not be conformed to this world, but be transformed by the renewal of your mind, that by testing you may discern what is the will of God, what is good and acceptable and perfect" (Romans 12:2). This transformation must take place daily.

The Guilt Trip

The moment you trust in Christ, a wonderful thing happens. You become identified with Christ. You become joined in spiritual union to Him. Because the Father accepts Christ perfectly, He also accepts you perfectly because you are in Christ. Notice the following verses (emphasis added):

> There is therefore now no condemnation for those who are *in Christ Jesus* (Romans 8:1).

> For I am sure that neither death nor life, nor angels nor rulers, nor things present nor things to come, nor powers, nor height nor depth, nor anything else in all creation, will be able to separate us from the love of God *in Christ Jesus our Lord* (Romans 8:38-39).

> Thanks be to God, who *in Christ* always leads us in triumphal procession (2 Corinthians 2:14).

> Therefore, if anyone is *in Christ*, he is a new creation. The old has passed away; behold, the new has come (2 Corinthians 5:17).

As we might expect, Satan seeks to blind the minds of Christians to this glorious and liberating truth. His goal is to keep us from focusing on our standing in Christ and focus instead on the need to do good works to earn God's favor. When we do not live up to the standards of God's law in the Bible, Satan then shifts his attention to accusing our consciences and making us feel like a worm before God. Satan is "the accuser of our brothers" (Revelation 12:10). He constantly accuses our conscience and wants us to feel guilt and despondency over our consistent failure to meet God's demands. As Clinton Arnold puts it, Satan "reminds believers of their shortcomings, unworthiness, and sin. By stimulating feelings of guilt, he hopes to keep Christians from feeling well-assured in their relationship to Christ and unworthy to receive his empowering grace."[9]

All this leads to a sense of alienation from God. If we think God has something against us because of a sin we've committed, it is natural for us to back off and alienate ourselves from Him (see Genesis 3:8).

Christians who succumb to this line of thinking have forgotten that they are *in Christ* and that the Father sees us as being *in Christ*. My friends, we must ever remind ourselves of this pivotal spiritual truth! It is a key component in our victory in spiritual warfare. (More on this later.)

The Affliction of Discouragement

I once read a story that depicted the devil having a garage sale. On the day of the sale, his tools were on open display for public inspection, each being marked with its sale price. There were many implements for sale, among them hatred, envy, jealousy, deceit, lust, lying, and pride.

Set apart from the rest was a harmless-looking tool. It had a lot of wear and tear and yet had a very high price.

"What is the name of this tool?" a customer asked, pointing to it.

"That is discouragement," Satan replied.

"Why have you priced it so high?"

"Because it is more useful to me than the others," Satan said. "I can pry open and get inside a man's heart with that, even when I cannot get near him with the other tools. It appears worn because I use it on almost everyone, since so few people know it belongs to me."

Be forewarned! Satan may attempt to use discouragement in your life to neutralize you as a Christian. "Satan would have us occupied with our difficulties and overcome with cares. Perhaps this is why Peter first tells us to cast all our cares upon God, assuring us of God's care, and then tells us to beware of our adversary the devil, who prowls about seeking whom he may devour (1 Peter 5:7-8)."[10]

Satan may seek to devour believers with persecution, personal rejection, a lack of appreciation by peers, and other things, all to generate discouragement. Only the act of casting all our cares upon God can nullify this expensive, effective tool of the devil.

Satan's Blueprint Against Christians in the End Times

Satan will use these tactics against Christians not only in the present age but also in the end times, during the tribulation period. He will be busy flinging the flaming darts of persecution, accompanied by the emotional pain such persecution causes (see Revelation 12:13,17). Some darts may be lethal, leading to martyrdom (Revelation 6:9-11). He will wear down the defenses of God's people. Satan—through his puppet antichrist—will "conquer" God's people (Revelation 13:7) and "prevail" over them (Daniel 7:21).

Satan will no doubt continue messing with the minds of God's people, afflicting them with guilt and discouragement during the tribulation period. As Christians continue to suffer persecution and even martyrdom, Satan may tempt some to wonder if God really cares for them. He may tempt some to wonder if suffering for Christ is really worth it. He may tempt some to think they're lousy Christians because their commitment is waning in the face of severe adversity. I believe this may be one reason God so often provides motivations for Christians to persevere in their commitment in the book of Revelation. For example:

> To the one who conquers I will grant to eat of the tree of life, which is in the paradise of God (Revelation 2:7).

> The one who conquers will not be hurt by the second death (2:11).

> To the one who conquers I will give some of the hidden manna, and I will give him a white stone, with a new name written on the stone that no one knows except the one who receives it (2:17).

> The one who conquers and who keeps my works until the end, to him I will give authority over the nations (2:26).

> The one who conquers will be clothed thus in white garments, and I will never blot his name out of the book of life (3:5).

> The one who conquers, I will make him a pillar in the temple of my God (3:12).

> The one who conquers, I will grant him to sit with me on my throne (3:21).

> These are the ones coming out of the great tribulation… They shall hunger no more, neither thirst anymore…For the Lamb in the midst of the throne will be their shepherd, and he will guide them to springs of living water, and God will wipe away every tear from their eyes (7:14-17).

> "Write this: Blessed are the dead who die in the Lord from now on." "Blessed indeed," says the Spirit, "that

they may rest from their labors, for their deeds follow them!" (14:13).

Behold, I am coming like a thief! Blessed is the one who stays awake (Revelation 16:15).

In the next chapter, I will continue my discussion of Satan's blueprint against Christians, focusing specifically on the flaming darts of depression, worry, anger, personal offense, and robbing us of joy.

5

SATAN'S SCHEMES:

Depression, Doubts, Worry, Anger, Personal Offense, and Robbing Joy

I n the previous chapter, I introduced Satan's schemes by summarizing what Scripture says about his flaming darts, his goal of bringing down your defenses, his attempt to mess with your mind, his goal of inflicting a guilt trip upon you, and his effective use of discouragement to attempt sending you into a tailspin. In this chapter, I zero in on Satan's flaming darts relating to depression, doubts, worry, anger, personal offense, and robbing your joy.

The Affliction of Depression

A favorite tactic of the devil is to generate depression in the heart of a Christian (see 1 Peter 5:6-8). D. Martyn Lloyd-Jones, who wrote *Spiritual Depression: Its Causes and Cures* (a book every

Christian should read), says, "There is no end to the ways in which the devil produces spiritual depression."[1] One of the more effective ways is to cause Christians to feel "not good enough" for God. Lloyd-Jones suggests that the cure for this variety of spiritual depression is relatively simple:

> Forget yourself, forget all about yourself. Of course you are not good enough, you never will be good enough…It does not matter what you have been, it does not matter what you have done…Look to Christ and to Christ alone and to nothing and no one else…The first thing you have to do is to say farewell now once and for ever to your past. Realize that it has been covered and blotted out in Christ. Never look back at your sins again. Say: "It is finished, it is covered by the Blood of Christ"…What you need is not to make resolutions to live a better life, to start fasting and sweating and praying. No! You just begin to say: "I rest my faith on Him alone Who died for my transgressions to atone."[2]

We should not interpret Lloyd-Jones as saying that living right is unimportant once you've become a Christian. He's saying that the ground of your acceptance before God has nothing to do with good works but everything to do with trusting in Christ, who took care of your sins at Calvary.

The primary goal is to maintain your position in Christ, the divine Savior. Feast your soul on Bible promises relating to being "in Christ." As noted in the previous chapter, Romans 8:1 affirms that "there is therefore now no condemnation for those who are *in Christ Jesus*." Second Corinthians 5:17 tells us, "Therefore, if anyone is *in Christ*, he is a new creation. The old has passed away; behold, the new has come." Galatians 3:26 tells us, "*In Christ Jesus* you are all sons of God, through faith." Romans 8:38-39 tells us, "For I am sure that neither death nor life, nor angels nor rulers, nor things present nor things to come, nor powers, nor height nor depth, nor anything else in all creation, will be able to separate us from the love of God *in Christ Jesus our Lord.*" As you rest serenely in your position "in Christ," spiritual depression lifts.

The Affliction of Doubts

Another tactic of the devil is to generate doubts in the heart of a Christian. To illustrate this, consider Genesis 3:1-5:

> Now the serpent was more crafty than any other beast of the field that the LORD God had made.
> He said to the woman, "Did God actually say, 'You shall not eat of any tree in the garden'?" And the woman said to the serpent, "We may eat of the fruit of the trees in the garden, but God said, 'You shall not eat of the fruit of the tree that is in the midst of the garden, neither shall you touch it, lest you die.'" But the serpent said to the woman, "You will not surely die. For God knows that when you eat of it your eyes will be opened, and you will be like God, knowing good and evil."

Satan successfully raised doubts in Eve's mind about God's Word and God's motives. After Eve succumbed to these doubts, she was easy prey for Satan, and this ultimately led to Adam's sin and the subsequent fall of humankind.

These days the devil loves to get Christians doubting God's grace (compare with Galatians 1:6-10). Perhaps he's tried this tactic on you. Have you ever felt like a horrible Christian because you know you're not good enough? Have you ever suffered discouragement because your life does not measure up to God's Word? Have you ever doubted your salvation? Have you ever doubted you're going to heaven because sin remains in your life? If so, there's a good possibility the devil has successfully generated doubts in your heart about God's grace.

Chip Ingram says the devil "specializes in casting doubt on the very basis of God's goodness and the means by which we receive it: *the gospel*. He always attacks grace." Ingram concedes that he himself struggled with this in his earlier years: "I was always doubting, always unsure, and always living with piles of condemnation and overwhelming guilt. I came close to giving up—in fact, I once officially decided to quit the Christian life—because I couldn't stand being a hypocrite."[3]

The only remedy for this satanic attack is to (1) drive a stake into the ground with the ironclad promises of God that our salvation rests *entirely* upon God's grace; and (2) remind ourselves daily that the ground of our acceptance before God is that we are "in Christ."

God's grace-gift of salvation permeates New Testament revelation: Acts 20:24 speaks of "the gospel of the grace of God." Ephesians 1:7 promises, "In him we have redemption through his blood, the forgiveness of our trespasses, according to the riches of his grace." Ephesians 2:8-9 affirms, "By grace you have been saved through faith. And this is not your own doing; it is the gift of God, not a result of works, so that no one may boast." Romans 3:24 assures us we "are justified by his grace as a gift, through the redemption that is in Christ Jesus" (see also Titus 3:7). Salvation is a grace-gift. It cannot be earned.

Because of what Christ accomplished on our behalf at the cross, the ground of our acceptance before God is that we are "in Christ." Those in Christ are "a new creation" (2 Corinthians 5:17), have "no condemnation" (Romans 8:1), and cannot be separated "from the love of God" (Romans 8:38-39).

The Affliction of Worry

Another common tactic of the devil centers on worry. I find it highly revealing that Peter speaks about worry and anxiety in the same context that he speaks of the devil: "Humble yourselves, therefore, under the mighty hand of God so that at the proper time he may exalt you, casting all your anxieties on him, because he cares for you. Be sober-minded; be watchful. Your adversary the devil prowls around like a roaring lion, seeking someone to devour" (1 Peter 5:6-8). Could it be that one way Satan seeks to devour us is by rousing worry in our lives? Could it be that one of the "flaming darts" Paul speaks of in Ephesians 6:16 is a dart of worry?

People often worry over two things: (1) the sins, wrongdoings, and failures of the past, and (2) fear of future failures, including monetary failures, failing health, and the fear of death. Notice the dilemma: *We worry in the present as we agonize over the past and the future.*

Satan especially loves to fill people with worry about death. But trusting in Jesus can dispel that worry: "Because God's children are human beings—made of flesh and blood—the Son also became flesh and blood. For only as a human being could he die, and only by dying could he break the power of the devil, who had the power of death. Only in this way could he set free all who have lived their lives as slaves to the fear of dying" (Hebrews 2:14-15 NLT). Jesus conquered death. He was raised from the dead. And those who trust in Him for salvation will likewise experience resurrection from the dead. One therefore need not fear death. It is a conquered foe.

As for more generalized worries about the future, Jesus, in the Sermon on the Mount, gives us a rather simple but profound instruction: "Do not be anxious about tomorrow, for tomorrow will be anxious for itself. Sufficient for the day is its own trouble" (Matthew 6:34). This means we should focus primarily on the *now*, not the past or the future. *Live in the present moment.* Live your life to the fullest each moment of every day, with a conscious awareness that God is with you at every step. Don't sweat the past. Don't sweat the future.

This doesn't mean we can't plan for the future. We can and we should. Just don't worry about it.

Satan also loves to get us worrying about things we cannot change. Robert Lightner observes that "one of the devil's tricks is to keep us so busy worrying about things we can do nothing about that we fail to do anything about the things we can change."[4] The best advice is to do all you can regarding the things you can change and leave the rest entirely in God's hands (see Proverbs 3:5-6).

The single best antidote to worry is prayer. The apostle Paul instructs, "Do not be anxious about anything, but in everything by prayer and supplication with thanksgiving let your requests be made known to God. And the peace of God, which surpasses all understanding, will guard your hearts and your minds in Christ Jesus" (Philippians 4:6-7). So, relieve your burden of worry by transferring it onto the shoulders of almighty God via prayer. "The peace of God, which surpasses all understanding" is like a sledgehammer that smashes the worried thoughts rooted in the devil.

Fanning Anger into Flame

I read that Corrie ten Boom was speaking at a church service in Munich when she beheld a former SS officer—one of her former prison guards—in the congregation. He came up to Corrie after the service and said, "How grateful I am for your message, Fraulein.

To think that, as you say, He has washed my sins away!" He thrust his hand out to shake her hand. She kept her hand at her side. How could she forgive him? Yet, as she pondered that Jesus had even died for this man—as she pondered Christ's call on her life—she prayed silently for the Lord to enable her to forgive him. After an immense inner struggle, she resolved to respond God's way and then sensed the love of Christ flooding her whole being. She reached out to a former enemy. She learned the truth that taking up one's cross is often very hard to do.[5]

Had Corrie ten Boom not forgiven the man, she could have held on to anger and allowed it to fester and grow into bitterness that could have eaten away at her like a cancer of the soul. That is a dangerous place to be. The apostle Paul thus warns us in Ephesians 4:26-27, "Be angry and do not sin; do not let the sun go down on your anger, and give no opportunity to the devil."

This verse tells us that there is such a thing as nonsinful anger. Corrie ten Boom's initial anger at seeing the former Nazi guard illustrates righteous anger. But had she held on to that anger, it could have become sinful had she let it fester in her heart, growing into bitterness, and this could have then given an opportunity to the devil. We must all guard against this.

Warren W. Wiersbe offers this wise warning:

> The believer who harbors bitterness and malice in his heart is giving Satan one of his most effective beachheads!...[Unforgiveness can] hinder the Spirit from working in our lives, and this robs us of the power we need to detect and defeat the devil. The old nature delights in breeding this kind of poison...The longer you harbor an unforgiving spirit, the more territory Satan will gain in your life.[6]

Unresolved anger, accompanied by bitterness and resentment, makes Jesus' words about forgiving others for their transgressions against us so very important. In Matthew 18:21-22 (NLT) we read: "Peter came to him and asked, 'Lord, how often should I forgive someone who sins against me? Seven times?' 'No, not seven times,' Jesus replied, 'but seventy times seven.'"

The Pharisees taught that righteousness demanded that a person forgive an offender two times. The Jewish rabbis taught that if one wanted to be magnanimous, one should forgive up to three times. When Peter asked Jesus about forgiving seven times, he no doubt thought he was being generous. Jesus went far beyond what Peter considered generous and urged, in essence, that we should forgive *without limit*.

This is especially the case since God has already forgiven us of our much more serious sins (see Matthew 18:23-35). I'm convinced that following Jesus' advice on forgiving others will help save us from many of the devil's onslaughts.

Provoking Personal Offense

Closely related to the danger of anger is taking offense at what others say or do to us. Whether it takes place in the family, among friends, at the workplace, or even at church, taking offense at others is a deadly trap by which Satan can ensnare us.

Taking offense injures the soul: "Offended people produce much fruit, such as hurt, anger, outrage, jealousy, resentment, strife, bitterness, hatred, and envy."[7] All of these can provide an opportunity for the devil to afflict us further (Ephesians 4:26-27).

It is probably correct to say that Christians who have taken offense at others fall into one of two categories:

(1) those who have been treated unjustly or (2) those who *believe* they have been treated unjustly...Often their conclusions are drawn from inaccurate information. Or their information is accurate, but their conclusion is distorted. Either way, they hurt, and their understanding is darkened. They judge by assumption, appearance, and hearsay.[8]

Once we feel offended, we view ourselves as victims. We then rationalize that we have every right to hold on to resentment and unforgiveness toward that person. The problem is, *resentment injures only one person: YOU.* Not only does resentment eat away at your soul like a spiritual cancer, but it can give an opportunity to the devil to wreak further havoc in your life. If you want to be victorious in spiritual warfare, you need to take the path of humility and let go of personal offenses. Meditate on 2 Timothy 2:24: "A servant of the Lord must not quarrel but must be kind to everyone" (NLT).

We must always be ready to forgive those who offend us. In Matthew 18:23-34, Jesus told a parable about forgiveness. He spoke of a master who commanded a servant to be sold along with his family to pay for the debt the servant owed (ten thousand talents, which would amount to several million dollars today). But then the master forgave the servant and cancelled the debt when the servant begged him to (verses 23-27).

The forgiven servant then found another servant who owed him a small amount of money he could not repay (one hundred denarii, or about sixteen dollars in today's economy). He would not forgive the debtor and threw him into prison (verses 28-30). When the other servants witnessed what happened, they reported it to the master (verse 31). The master then ordered the wicked servant to be punished until he repaid all his debts (verses 32-34).

After telling this story, Jesus said, "This is how my heavenly Father will treat each of you unless you forgive your brother or sister from your heart" (Matthew 18:35 NIV). We each need to realize we are incapable of paying the debt we owe to God. We are morally indebted to God because of our sin. Each of us is like the man who had an insurmountable debt he could not repay. God has freely forgiven us as Christians of all indebtedness. We are thus obliged to forgive others who wrong us because their wrongs are a mere pittance compared with the countless wrongs we've committed against God and for which we have received forgiveness.

Perhaps I can put it this way: God calls us to forgive others for their petty crimes against us because the Lord has already forgiven our much greater capital crimes against Him that deserve the death penalty.

It all comes down to this—forgiving others has a triple benefit:

1. It pleases the Lord.

2. It heals our emotions in the face of personal offense.

3. It thwarts the efforts of the devil in our life.

Forgiving others is a no-brainer!

Robbing Your Joy

There is a corollary tactic Satan often uses with his other tactics. Whether Satan seeks to induce guilt, discouragement, depression, doubts, worry, anger, or taking personal offense, his goal is to *rob you of your joy in the Lord*.

Satan already knows he can't take away your salvation. But he'll try to take away your joy of salvation. He knows that if he can take away your joy, he can make you weak as a Christian. Nehemiah 8:10

tells us "the joy of the Lord is your strength." Conversely, losing that joy depletes our spiritual strength.

This satanic strategy can be nullified by anchoring yourself *unconditionally* on the Word of God, believing *every word* on *every page*. George Müller, one of the great prayer and faith warriors in recent church history, spoke about his habit every single morning upon arising:

> The first great and primary business to which I ought to attend every day was, to have my soul happy in the Lord. The first thing to be concerned about was not, how much I might serve the Lord, how I might glorify the Lord; but how I might get my soul into a happy state, and how my inner man may be nourished...I saw that the most important thing I had to do was to give myself to the reading of the Word of God and to meditation on it.[9]

I think Müller embodied the truth of Psalm 1:1-2 (NLT): "Oh, the joys of those who...delight in the law of the Lord, meditating on it day and night." This practice gave Müller not only inner happiness and joy but also increased his faith mightily. You and I would be wise to follow his lead.

Satan's Blueprint Against Christians in the End Times

Satan will continue to use these tactics against Christians not only in the present age but also in the end times, during the tribulation period. He will be busy flinging the flaming darts of depression, doubts, worry, anger, taking personal offense, and robbing believers of joy.

Christians during the tribulation period will experience great persecution and martyrdom (Matthew 24:8-9; Mark 13:9-11,13;

Luke 21:12-17; 2 Timothy 3:1-5,10-13; Revelation 6:9-11; 12:17; 16:6; 20:4). Food will be minimal, due not only to widespread famine (Revelation 6:8; 18:8), but also because Christians will refuse to receive the mark of the beast, thereby preventing them from being able to buy or sell (Revelation 13:17). During this time, Christians will be "hated by all nations" (Matthew 24:9).

It's hard enough for individual Christians to suffer through all this. It's even harder for Christians to witness their own family members and friends also suffering through it. Tribulation saints will experience grief piled upon grief. This being the case, we can easily see how Christians in the tribulation period will be a "target-rich environment" for the devil's flaming darts.

In the next chapter, I'll continue my exposé on Satan's blueprint against Christians, focusing specifically on inciting pride in the heart, hindering answers to prayer, tempting to sin, and causing division among God's people.

6

SATAN'S SCHEMES:

Pride, Hindering Prayer, Sin, and Causing Division

heard a preacher say to his congregation, "I was planning on speaking on humility this morning, but I will save that message for a larger audience." I laughed at the joke, but pride is no laughing matter.

Puffing Up with Pride

We recall from chapter 2 that the sin that corrupted Lucifer was self-generated pride. Ezekiel 28:15 tells us that Lucifer was perfect in his ways until unrighteousness surfaced in him. God describes this unrighteousness in verse 17: "Your heart was proud because of your beauty; you corrupted your wisdom for the sake of your splendor." Lucifer became so impressed with his own beauty, brilliance, intelligence, power, and position that he began to desire for himself the honor and glory that belonged to God alone.

As we saw earlier, Lucifer's five "I wills" in Isaiah 14:13-14 high-light his pride:

> You said in your heart,
>   "I will ascend to heaven;
> above the stars of God
>   I will set my throne on high;
> I will sit on the mount of assembly
>   in the far reaches of the north;
> I will ascend above the heights of the clouds;
>   I will make myself like the Most High."

God had no choice but to judge Lucifer. God cast him from heaven down to the earth (Ezekiel 28:16), exiling him from the heavenly government and his place of authority (see Luke 10:18). His name then changed from Lucifer ("morning star") to Satan ("adversary").

Just as Satan fell through pride, so he seeks for Christians to fall through pride. We see many examples in Scripture of Satan tempting through pride:

- Part of Satan's temptation of Eve was, "You will be like God" (Genesis 3:5).

- Part of Satan's influence on David to take a census of fighting men in Israel related to David's pride at the strength of his forces.

- Satan even tried to tempt Jesus through human pride: "The devil took him to a very high mountain and showed him all the kingdoms of the world and their glory. And he said to him, 'All these I will give you, if you will fall down and worship me'" (Matthew 4:8-9).

Scripture understandably warns that "a church leader must not be a new believer, because he might become proud, and the devil would cause him to fall" (1 Timothy 3:6 NLT). It is no wonder that Peter speaks of the need for humility in the same context as speaking about the devil: "Humble yourselves, therefore, under the mighty hand of God so that at the proper time he may exalt you, casting all your anxieties on him, because he cares for you. Be sober-minded; be watchful. Your adversary the devil prowls around like a roaring lion, seeking someone to devour" (1 Peter 5:6-8).

In truth, pride lies at the very heart of the choice to sin. Whenever we disobey God's will, we are displaying pride and independence.[1] Jim Logan says that pride involves "setting you and me up as the final authorities in our lives, deciding for ourselves what's right and wrong for us. That's taking God's place in our lives, and He hates it."[2]

Choosing humility does not mean you purposefully think lowly thoughts about yourself ("I'm no good; I'm unworthy"). Rather, it means you do not think of yourself *at all*. The humble person recognizes that all he or she has comes from God: "A person cannot receive even one thing unless it is given him from heaven" (John 3:27). "What do you have that you did not receive?" (1 Corinthians 4:7).

Pride is dangerous ground to tread upon: "God opposes the proud but gives grace to the humble" (1 Peter 5:5). "Everyone who is arrogant in heart is an abomination to the LORD" (Proverbs 16:5). "Pride goes before destruction, and a haughty spirit before a fall" (Proverbs 16:18). "One's pride will bring him low" (Proverbs 29:23).

Pride can bring swift divine discipline. Randy Alcorn comments, "Acting in arrogance is like wearing a sign that says 'kick me.' Being proud is a prayer to God: 'strike me down.' It's a prayer He's certain

to answer. Every day, every hour, we choose either to humble ourselves or to be proud."[3]

My friend, choose humility! You'll please God and defeat the
devil.

Hindering Answered Prayer

I noted previously that God sometimes dispatches holy angels
to take part in bringing answers to our prayers. When Christians
prayed to God on behalf of Peter while he was in jail, for example,
God arranged a jailbreak through an angel (Acts 12:6-19).

Scripture also reveals that fallen angels can sometimes thwart
the efforts of holy angels who are involved in answering prayers. An
example is found in Daniel 10:13, where a fallen angel detained a
holy angel God sent to take care of Daniel's prayer request. It is good
to remember that there are different ranks among God's holy angels
and the fallen angels (Ephesians 6:12; Colossians 1:16). The demonic
spirit that stood against God's holy angel must have been a high-
ranking fallen angel, working under Satan's command.

Only when the archangel Michael showed up to render aid
was the lesser angel freed to carry out his task. Michael is the only
archangel mentioned in the Bible. *Archangel* implies a rank of first
among angels. Apparently, Michael is in authority over all the other
holy angels, including the thrones, dominions, rulers, and authorities mentioned in Colossians 1:16. He is exceedingly powerful, more
than a match for any demonic spirit.

Here's the important lesson to remember: We must remain fervent in our prayers and not think God is ignoring us because there
seems to be a delay in His answer. You never know what's going on
behind the scenes—especially in relation to spiritual warfare. Keep
your faith strong. And keep those prayers flowing.

Minimizing Sin

The devil will do anything he can to entice you to take a minimalist view of sin. The lighter the view of sin in your heart, the better Satan likes it.

Satan may try to minimize your view of sin by twisting God's Word. To Eve he said, "Did God actually say…?" (Genesis 3:1). This ultimately led to Adam's sin, followed by the fall of humankind.

Seventeenth-century author William Gurnall suggests that the devil may try to convince you that little sins don't matter too much: "When the Spirit convicts you of sin, Satan will try to convince you, 'It is such a little one—spare it.'"[4] Satan may whisper to your mind's ear: "This sin is so minor. It's no big deal. Don't trouble yourself. It will be of no consequence. You're fine. Go ahead."

What such a view does not recognize is that if you give the devil an inch, he'll try to take a mile. John Owen, a seventeenth-century church leader, was correct in affirming, "A former experience of sin is an advantage Satan uses to make another, more spectacular assault. Without the previous entry of sin, the greater assault is not possible."[5] So beware of small compromises.

Another way Satan can make Christians feel okay about sin is by causing them to have a distorted view of God's grace. He might entice them to think God's grace is a license to sin. Jude 1:4 speaks of ungodly people who "pervert the grace of our God into sensuality and deny our only Master and Lord, Jesus Christ." Paul asked, "Are we to sin because we are not under law but under grace? By no means!" (Romans 6:15). Thomas Watson (1620–1686), a Puritan preacher, warned, "Take heed of abusing this mercy of God…To sin because mercy abounds is the devil's logic."[6]

Knowing the fallenness and propensity toward sin in the human heart, the devil might sometimes lighten his temptations for a short time to produce a level of prideful self-confidence in the Christian ("I'm really being victorious today!"). He then waits for the sin nature to produce its inevitable fruit—heinous sin. As J.I. Packer put it, "Sin is always at work in the heart; a temporary lull in its assaults means not that it is dead, but that it is very much alive...Sin's strategy is to induce a false sense of security as a prelude to a surprise attack."[7] When that surprise attack occurs, Satan moves in as the tempter and seeks to fan it into flame, bringing as much ruination as possible to the unsuspecting Christian.

Christian beware!

Seduction to Sexual Sin

The apostle Paul, in addressing sexuality within the marriage relationship, warned his readers: "Do not deprive one another, except perhaps by agreement for a limited time, that you may devote yourselves to prayer; but then come together again, so that Satan may not tempt you because of your lack of self-control" (1 Corinthians 7:5). When self-control is lacking, a Christian is easy prey for Satan's seduction to sexual sin.

It grieves me to say it, but this has become an immense problem in the Christian church today. Hands down, this is Satan's most successful tactic in bringing massive numbers of Christians into bondage.

One evidence of this is that Christian pastors are frequently peeking at pornography. The Barna Group surveyed some 432 pastors and 338 youth pastors. "Most pastors (57%) and youth pastors (64%) admit they have struggled with porn, either currently or in the past," Barna reported. "Overall, 21 percent of youth pastors and 14 percent of pastors admit they currently struggle with using porn."[8] The survey also revealed that over one in ten youth pastors (12 percent) and one in twenty pastors (5 percent) say they are "addicted" to porn.

Not unexpectedly, 75 percent of youth pastors and 64 percent of pastors said looking at porn has negatively impacted their ministries. And 87 percent of the pastors said they felt shame about their viewing habits, with 55 percent affirming they lived in constant fear of others finding out about it.[9]

Also alarming is the rising number of females looking at porn today. *Christianity Today* reports that "porn addiction is typically seen as a male problem, both in the church and society. The majority of porn addiction resources are directed at men, but awareness is growing that it isn't just a guy thing."[10] Statistics reveal that 20 percent of Christian women admit addiction to pornography. Among college-age women, 18 percent admit to spending time on the Internet viewing sexual images.[11] One study found that one in three visitors to porn websites are women, and that 9.4 million women access porn monthly.[12] Understandably, 70 percent of women keep their porn use a secret. Tragically, the Internet has become "a great accelerator for pornography because it is accessible, affordable, and anonymous."[13]

An added tragedy is that viewing porn can have a traumatic effect on marriage and the family. God designed sex to be one of the sweet and intimate joys of lifelong marriage (Genesis 2:24; Matthew 19:5; 1 Timothy 4:4; Hebrews 13:4; see also the Song of Solomon). Young people whose minds feed on porn prior to marriage will find it difficult to experience sexual satisfaction with their spouse. Likewise, a married man or woman who feeds on porn will find it difficult to experience sexual satisfaction with his or her spouse. Porn has a strong desensitizing effect. The more porn one feeds on, the more desensitized one becomes to sexual stimulation. No spouse can compete with the graphic and highly stimulating sexual images and videos on the Internet. Marriage and the family are innocent victims in the world of porn.

Regretfully, many today—even within the Christian church—take a permissive view of sex before marriage. In 2016, Bromleigh McCleneghan published a book titled *Good Christian Sex: Why Chastity Isn't the Only Option—and Other Things the Bible Says About Sex*. McCleneghan argues that premarital sex is okay for Christians: "We can be chaste—faithful—in unmarried sexual relationships if we exercise restraint: if we refrain from having sex that isn't mutually pleasurable and affirming."[14]

Many reviewers love McCleneghan's book. *The Washington Post* says, "McCleneghan argues against a rule-based look at biblical purity and opens up the scripture to a more holistic approach." *Publisher's Weekly* says, "McCleneghan offers ways to rethink biblical passages and find a compromise so that faith and embracing human sexuality don't have to be mutually exclusive." A rabbi commented, "*Good Christian Sex* shows what open-minded, sex-positive encounters with the holy can and should look like." An article in the *Religion News Service* says, "What you thought was naughty may actually be holy. That's the message of *Good Christian Sex*, Bromleigh McCleneghan's attempt to free Christians from shame about having premarital or extramarital sex."[15]

McCleneghan consistently engages in *eisegesis* (reading meanings into biblical texts that are not there) instead of *exegesis* (objectively drawing the meaning out of the text of Scripture itself). McCleneghan has decided in advance what Scripture should say, and then "interprets" Scripture to say that very thing.

Correctly understood, the pages of Scripture reveal that marriage is a divinely ordered institution designed to form a permanent union between one man and one woman, not only to bring blessing to each other but also to procreate the human race (see Genesis 1:27-28; 2:24). The Lord Jesus Himself gave support for God's design for marriage (Matthew 19:4-5).

Scripture is consistent in its emphasis that a sexual relationship can be engaged in *only* within the confines of marriage—that is, a marriage between a male and a female (1 Corinthians 7:2). The apostles urged all Christians to abstain from fornication (Acts 15:20). The apostle Paul said that the body is not for fornication and that a person should flee it (1 Corinthians 6:13,18).

Sex within a biblically defined marriage, however, is very good. Sex was a part of God's "good" creation. God created sex and "everything God created is good" (1 Timothy 4:4 NLT). But it is good *only* within the confines of the marriage relationship, which He Himself ordained (see Hebrews 13:4).

A key component in overcoming sexual sin is to walk in dependence upon the Holy Spirit. In Galatians 5:16-17, the apostle Paul says, "Walk by the Spirit, and you will not gratify the desires of the flesh. For the desires of the flesh are against the Spirit, and the desires of the Spirit are against the flesh, for these are opposed to each other, to keep you from doing the things you want to do." The works of the flesh include "sexual immorality, impurity, [and] sensuality" (verse 19). The fruit of the Holy Spirit includes "self-control" (verse 23). This means that the person who walks in dependence upon the Holy Spirit receives supernatural help in maintaining self-control in the face of sexual temptations. There's no way you'll be victorious in your own strength.

Though sexual immorality, impurity, and sensuality are works of the fallen flesh (Galatians 5:19), demonic spirits can fan all these into a much more passionate flame. Merrill F. Unger thus warns:

A believer with a tendency toward lascivious thoughts yields to the temptation to indulge the old nature by reading pornographic literature. He soon finds his mind polluted by vile imaginations whenever he attempts to read the Bible or pray or perform any spiritual service for God. Strong demonic influence on his mind stifles every effort in Christian living and serving…The lascivious tendency grows into an overpowering obsession as unclean thoughts overmaster the mind. Open immorality or sexual perversion is the result, and ministry and witness for God are destroyed.[16]

Do not give up, however, for there is hope in the pages of Scripture. We not only gain self-control by walking in dependence on the Holy Spirit, we also find unlimited resources in combatting fleshly temptations and the powers of darkness in discovering our true identity in Christ. Tony Evans expands on this important truth:

You are a saint—washed, sanctified, and justified. You have a new identity now. When you keep that truth at the forefront of your mind, eventually the craving for whatever behavior you were doing will begin to have less and less control over you because it does not line up with who you are. You will be functioning first and foremost out of your identity in Christ.[17]

I've already introduced our identity "in Christ" in the last few chapters, but I'll address it in much greater detail later in the book. For now, I urge you to resist Satan's implanted thought that "there is no hope for you because you're a sexual pervert." Christians are finding sexual freedom in Christ every single day. So keep your hope alive. Deliverance is available and sustainable.

Divide and Conquer

Yet another tactic Satan has in his arsenal is the time-tested strategy of *divide and conquer* (see 1 Corinthians 1:10-11; 3:1-9; 5:2; 6:1; 8:1-13; 2 Corinthians 2:10-11). I've visited Christian ministries where there was a great deal of infighting, heightened resentments, people arguing and not getting along, unresolved offenses, and, on one occasion, a fistfight nearly breaking out until I lodged myself between the two men and urged them to separate from each other and decompress. (*How bold of me!*) Today this ministry is a faint reflection of the powerful organization it once was. Satan successfully divided and conquered.

Satan is a master at causing division in churches, Christian fellowships, Bible studies, small discipleship groups, Christian companies, and personal friendships. Here is something you can count on: Where there is a lack of forgiveness in any Christian organization, there will be a corresponding weakening of that organization. This sad reality has caused David Jeremiah to warn that Satan

> injects the poisons of suspicion and intolerance and hatred and jealousy and criticism—poisons that seek an outlet in the body of Christ. Oftentimes that outlet is the human tongue: our words. James says the tongue "is set on fire by hell…It is an unruly evil, full of deadly poison" (James 3:6,8 NKJV). When we find hurtful words creating division in the church, guess who is delighted?[18]

Christian beware!

Satan's Blueprint Against Christians in the End Times

Satan will continue to use these tactics against Christians not only in the present age but also in the end times, during the tribulation period. He will be busy flinging the flaming darts of pride and arrogance, trying to hinder answers to prayer, seeking to minimize sin in the minds of Christians, tempting them to sexual sin, and inciting divisions among Christians. Such flaming darts will stand all the more chance of success in an environment (the tribulation period) characterized by rebellion against God, immorality, a lack of resources to meet basic human needs, and an ever-escalating resentment and hatred of all Christians.

In the next chapter, I provide even further insights on Satan's blueprint against Christians, with a specific focus on how he can hinder you through other people, cause bodily illness, attack churches, and promote apostasy.

7

SATAN'S SCHEMES:

Hindering Through Other People, Bodily Illness, Attacking Churches, and Apostasy

I noted in chapter 4 that Satan is relentless. He never gives up. If one tactic doesn't work against you, he'll quickly try another. By so doing, Satan seeks to wear down your defenses so you end up defeated. He will patiently keep coming after you. You, in turn, must be just as persistent in resisting him (James 4:7; 1 Peter 5:7-9). Following are a few more of his favorite strategies.

Working Through Other People to Hinder You

Satan can pester or hinder you through the words or actions of other people—sometimes including people who are closest to you. We see this illustrated in Peter, whom Satan influenced to hinder Christ's mission of dying on the cross for the salvation of humankind:

> Jesus began to show his disciples that he must go to Jerusalem and suffer many things from the elders and chief priests and scribes, and be killed, and on the third day be raised. And Peter took him aside and began to rebuke him, saying, "Far be it from you, Lord! This shall never happen to you." But he turned and said to Peter, "Get behind me, Satan! You are a hindrance to me. For you are not setting your mind on the things of God, but on the things of man" (Matthew 16:21-23).

In other cases, Satan or demonic spirits might work through a perfect stranger to hinder you. Acts 16:16-18 records how this happened to the apostle Paul:

> As we were going to the place of prayer, we were met by a slave girl who had a spirit of divination and brought her owners much gain by fortune-telling. She followed Paul and us, crying out, "These men are servants of the Most High God, who proclaim to you the way of salvation." And this she kept doing for many days. Paul, having become greatly annoyed, turned and said to the spirit, "I command you in the name of Jesus Christ to come out of her." And it came out that very hour.

We are also told that Satan "entered into" Judas, after which Judas betrayed Jesus (Luke 22:3; John 13:27). Satan also "filled" Ananias's heart to lie to Peter and to the Holy Spirit (Acts 5:3).

No doubt the most blatant example of Satan working through a person to hinder God's people is when he will empower the antichrist in all of his wicked deeds during the tribulation period: "The coming of the lawless one [the antichrist] is by the activity of Satan with all power and false signs and wonders" (2 Thessalonians 2:9). Revelation 13:2 reveals that Satan will give to the antichrist "his power and his throne and great authority." Satan will work through the puppet antichrist to harass, persecute, and even kill countless Christians during this time.

Such scriptural facts motivated Bible scholar John Phillips to warn, "We must see beyond people. Satan may use people to persecute us, lie to us, cheat us, hurt us...But our real enemy lurks in the shadows of the unseen world."[1]

We must act with discernment in all this. We must not assume that every time someone says something hurtful to us or hinders us, a demon is the culprit. It is unlikely we will know the specific involvements of Satan and demons regarding people who pester and hinder us. The exception might be a person who incessantly opposes an important work of ministry. Even then, we cannot know for sure.

Since this is the case, I suggest a fivefold safety protocol:

1. Keep your spiritual armor of God on.

2. Stand strong in your position in Christ.

3. Walk in dependence on the Holy Spirit.

4. Pray continually.

5. If you suspect demonic opposition through a particular person, then ask God to get involved in the situation.

Bodily Ailments

Aside from injuring Christians emotionally and relationally, Satan can also cause physical ailments in our bodies. Consider Job 2:1-7:

There was a day when the sons of God came to present themselves before the Lord, and Satan also came among them to present himself before the Lord. And the Lord said to Satan, "From where have you come?" Satan answered the Lord and said, "From going to and fro on the earth, and from walking up and down on it." And the Lord said to Satan, "Have you considered my servant Job, that there is none like him on the earth, a blameless and upright man, who fears God and turns away from evil? He still holds fast his integrity, although you incited me against him to destroy him without reason." Then Satan answered the Lord and said, "Skin for skin! All that a man has he will give for his life. But stretch out your hand and touch his bone and his flesh, and he will curse you to your face." And the Lord said to Satan, "Behold, he is in your hand; only spare his life."

So Satan went out from the presence of the Lord and struck Job with loathsome sores from the sole of his foot to the crown of his head.

Job was "blameless and upright" (Job 1:1). He had done nothing wrong. And yet God permitted Satan to cause sores up and down his body. God put limits on Satan, preventing Satan from taking Job's life. But God permitted the physical affliction.

The apostle Paul, too, suffered bodily affliction by a demon. We read in 2 Corinthians 12:7 (NLT), "So to keep me from becoming proud, I was given a thorn in my flesh, a messenger from Satan to torment me and keep me from becoming proud." The word *flesh* is the normal word in the Greek language used to denote the physical substance of the body. Whatever Paul suffered from, it was apparently a physical, bodily ailment. Some biblical scholars speculate that Paul had a painful eye disease.

The Greek word for *thorn* means "sharpened wooden shaft," "a stake," or "a splinter." This apparently was no little prick. Paul had to endure a serious and grievous suffering for an extended time. Paul prayed to the Lord three times to remove it, but God allowed Paul to retain it to keep him humble.

This affliction tormented Paul. The Greek word for *torment* literally means "to strike," "to beat," "to harass," or "to trouble." This is the same word used for the soldiers violently striking and beating Jesus during His trial (Matthew 26:67). Paul's physical ailment was beating him down. Despite this, God's response to Paul's request for the thorn's removal was *no*. This refusal on God's part was not in any way related to a sin or lack of faith on Paul's part. The affliction was not for *punishment* but for *protection*—that is, protection from a self-inflated attitude. Because of this, Paul accepted without hesitation God's verdict on the matter. While the affliction made him weak, Christ's strong power was all the more manifested through him.

While God has His providential reasons for allowing physical suffering, Satan also has his motives. The devil would love nothing more than to injure or destroy your physical body. The apostle Paul informs us in 1 Corinthians 6:19-20: "Do you not know that your body is a temple of the Holy Spirit within you, whom you have from God? You are not your own, for you were bought with a price. So glorify God in your body." Paul expressed his desire that "Christ will be honored in my body" (Philippians 1:20). In Romans 6:12-13 (NLT) Paul says of the mortal body: "Do not let sin control the way you live; do not give in to sinful desires. Do not let any part of your body become an instrument of evil to serve sin. Instead, give yourselves completely to God, for you were dead, but now you have new life. So use your whole body as an instrument to do what is right for the glory of God."

Here's the point: Satan attacks you not only because he hates you as a follower of Christ, but because he hates the Holy Spirit, and he doesn't want you to honor God in your body.

Further, Satan may seek to hinder world evangelism by afflicting the bodies of Christians. Warren Wiersbe suggests that "God wants to use your body as a vehicle for revealing him to a lost world...This means that when Satan attacks your body, he is attacking the one means God has of revealing his grace and love to a lost world."[2] The more Christians who have bodily afflictions, the more Satan can slow down world evangelism.

This means it is a divine imperative that we take care of our bodies. Go to the doctor when you're sick and visit the dentist when you need to. Try to eat healthy foods and get in some exercise. Stay fit for your service to God.

Aside from that rather obvious advice, I'm sure you're now also getting the picture that we face a serious battle when it comes to spiritual warfare. Satan seeks to injure you not only spiritually but also relationally, emotionally, and bodily. It's an all-out war. And you've got a big target on your back.

Attacking Christian Churches

Yet another tactic of the devil is direct attacks against Christian churches. Second Corinthians 11:14-15 reveals that "Satan disguises himself as an angel of light. So it is no surprise if his servants, also, disguise themselves as servants of righteousness." Some of these so-called "servants of righteousness" are preaching from Christian pulpits, spreading doctrinal confusion and even heresy. We also read in 1 Timothy 4:1, "The Holy Spirit tells us clearly that in the last times some will turn away from the true faith; they will follow deceptive spirits and teachings that come from demons" (NLT).

Who can deny that even today we are witnessing preachers teaching patently false ideas? Some deny that God is all-powerful or all-knowing. Some deny that Jesus was God on earth, and claim He even made mistakes when He was on earth. Some deny Jesus is the only way of salvation. Some claim the Bible is inspired just as Shakespeare is inspired—that is, it's inspiring to read, but it's a manmade book with mistakes. Some claim that the second coming takes place whenever a person finds God again in his or her heart. My friend, many in our day have departed from the faith once for all handed down to the saints (Jude 3). These are "teachings that come from demons" (1 Timothy 4:1 NLT).

Meanwhile, good churches are engaging in evangelistic efforts by spreading the Word of God in their communities. At the same time, Satan and the powers of darkness are busy trying to thwart those efforts. Jesus tells a parable about this in Mark 4:14-20 (NLT), in which He compares planting seeds to sharing the Word of God:

> The farmer plants seed by taking God's word to others. The seed that fell on the footpath represents those who hear the message, only to have Satan come at once and take it away. The seed on the rocky soil represents those who hear the message and immediately receive it with joy. But since they don't have deep roots, they don't last long. They fall away as soon as they have problems or are persecuted for believing God's word. The seed that fell among the thorns represents others who hear God's word, but all too quickly the message is crowded out by the worries of this life, the lure of wealth, and the desire for other things, so no fruit is produced. And the seed that fell on good soil represents those who hear and accept God's word and produce a harvest of thirty, sixty, or even a hundred times as much as had been planted!

There are many lessons in this parable. An important one is that the devil is busy trying to thwart the effect of the Word of God as it goes out to local communities. Satan and his fallen angels will do anything they can to prevent new people from leaving the kingdom of darkness and entering the kingdom of light—the kingdom of Jesus Christ. All the while, "Satan, who is the god of this world, has blinded the minds of those who don't believe. They are unable to see the glorious light of the Good News" (2 Corinthians 4:4 NLT).

Satan and his fallen angels can also instigate persecution against Christian churches. We think of Revelation 2:8-10, where Christ warned the church in Smyrna of satanic persecution that would cause some of them to go to prison and even become martyrs. In some parts of the world today, we are witnessing this happening. Especially in Muslim-dominated countries, such attacks on Christian congregations are all too common.

Satan and demons also have the power to prevent Christian service from taking place. A good example is in 1 Thessalonians 2:18, where the apostle Paul informed the Thessalonian Christians, "We wanted to come to you—I, Paul, again and again—but Satan hindered us." We do not know how this hindering took place, but somehow, some way, Satan thwarted Paul's efforts in ministry. Satan and demons can do the same today. These are days for discernment.

Lies, Deception, and Apostasy

We already know Satan is a deceiver. Satan deceived Adam and Eve in the Garden of Eden (Genesis 3:1-7). Paul later warned the Corinthian Christians: "I am afraid that as the serpent deceived Eve by his cunning, your thoughts will be led astray from a sincere and pure devotion to Christ" (2 Corinthians 11:3). Satan "does not stand in the truth, because there is no truth in him. When he lies, he speaks out of his own character, for he is a liar and the father of lies" (John 8:44). In his deception, Satan "disguises himself as an angel of light" (2 Corinthians 11:14). Satan is "the deceiver of the whole world" (Revelation 12:9; see also 20:10). He is also "the god of this world" who "has blinded the minds of the unbelievers" (2 Corinthians 4:4).

Such verses give us a clue that Satan and his army of fallen angels are behind the massive apostasy that has engulfed churches around the world. This seems to be one of Satan's primary tactics today. The apostle Paul knew that even among the New Testament churches, apostasy was a real and present danger. He therefore warned the elders in the church at Ephesus: "I know that after my departure fierce wolves will come in among you, not sparing the flock; and from among your own selves will arise men speaking twisted things, to draw away the disciples after them. Therefore be alert, remembering that for three years I did not cease night or day to admonish every one with tears" (Acts 20:29-31).

Scripture prophesies that great apostasy will emerge in the last days. In 1 Timothy 4:1 Paul warns: "Now the Spirit expressly says that in later times some will depart from the faith by devoting themselves to deceitful spirits and teachings of demons." False prophets propagate these teachings of demons. That is why 1 John 4:1 warns us, "Beloved, do not believe every spirit, but test the spirits to see whether they are from God, for many false prophets have gone out into the world."

The apostle Paul also speaks about apostasy in the last days in 2 Timothy 4:3-4: "The time is coming when people will not endure sound teaching, but having itching ears they will accumulate for themselves teachers to suit their own passions, and will turn away from listening to the truth and wander off into myths." Paul provides some specifics about this last-days apostasy in 2 Timothy 3:1-5:

> Understand this, that in the last days there will come times of difficulty. For people will be lovers of self, lovers of money, proud, arrogant, abusive, disobedient to their parents, ungrateful, unholy, heartless, unappeasable, slanderous, without self-control, brutal, not loving good, treacherous, reckless, swollen with conceit, lovers of pleasure rather than lovers of God, having the appearance of godliness, but denying its power. Avoid such people.

Lovers of self is just another way of describing the philosophy of humanism. *Lovers of money* is just another way of describing materialism. *Lovers of pleasure* is just another way of describing hedonism. It is significant that humanism, materialism, and hedonism are three of the most prominent philosophies in our world today, and they often go together. All this is a part of last-days apostasy.

Scripture reveals specific ways that people can apostatize. Included are a denial of God (2 Timothy 3:4-5), a denial of Christ (1 John 2:18), a denial of Christ's return (2 Peter 3:3-4), a denial of the faith (1 Timothy 4:1-2), a denial of sound doctrine (2 Timothy 4:3-4), a denial of morals (2 Timothy 3:1-8), and a denial of authority (2 Timothy 3:4). Even within the Christian church, I have witnessed every one of these denials over the past decade. I hate to say it, but some rather famous Christian leaders and authors have communicated rank heresy in some of their teachings. We are living in days of deception!

Today pastors are leaving not only their congregations, they are leaving the Christian faith altogether. Specialized websites now exist that help such pastors come out as unbelievers. An example is the

Clergy Project. This website claims to be an online community for active and former clergy who no longer subscribe to supernatural beliefs. It helps members "move beyond" their former faith, and aids them in how to tell family members that they no longer believe.

Another example is the website *Recovering from Religion.* This website aims to help people who no longer subscribe to any form of religion but who are still suffering some "aftereffects" of their former faith. It is a support community for people as they let go of their former religious beliefs.[3]

While many pastors are bailing on Christianity, many Christians who remain in the church have plummeted into mysticism. Many believers today derive their "truth" not from the Scriptures but from feelings and experience. People seem to yearn for a mystical-based spirituality as opposed to a fact-based faith.

In keeping with this, we are witnessing within Christian churches such things as deep breathing, Yoga, chanting, the use of mantras, and contemplative prayer. Contemplative prayer has as its goal a sense of union with God or oneness with God. We reportedly let go of conscious thoughts and immerse ourselves in the divine.

Mysticism in place of the objective Word of God is a fast track to apostasy. No longer does the Word of God function as a barometer of truth. Rather, feelings and experiences reign supreme.

Apostasy is not only alive and well today, it is thriving in abundance. It will get even worse as we near the end times. These are days for discernment as Satan and his host of fallen angels continue to deceive so many.

Satan's Blueprint Against Christians in the End Times

During the future tribulation period, Satan will continue to fling the flaming darts of lies, deception, apostasy, attacking churches, causing bodily illnesses, and much more. As an example, consider the escalation of deception during the tribulation period. Jesus, in His description of this period, said that "many false prophets will arise and lead many astray" (Matthew 24:11). We are also told that the antichrist will engage in unparalleled deception of the masses: "He will use every kind of evil deception to fool those on their way to destruction" (2 Thessalonians 2:10 NLT). The deception that flows out of the one-world religion associated with New Babylon will also be enormous (Revelation 17–18). Satan will be behind all of it, for he is "the father of lies" (John 8:44).

Just as some Christians are being deceived by false teachers today, so it is understandable that some who become Christians during the tribulation period will suffer some level of deception. We witness deception among a few of the seven churches of Revelation 2–3. For example, Jesus informed the church in Pergamum, "You have some there who hold the teaching of Balaam…So also you have some who hold the teaching of the Nicolaitans. Therefore repent" (Revelation 2:14-16). To the church in Thyatira, Jesus warned, "You tolerate that woman Jezebel, who calls herself a prophetess and is teaching and seducing my servants to practice sexual immorality and to eat food sacrificed to idols" (2:20). God's people have always been endangered through false prophets and false teachers. The same will no doubt be true during the tribulation period.

It is likely that during the oppressive years of persecution and martyrdom in the tribulation period, the church will go underground—meeting in stealth locations as opposed to church buildings. This means Satan will probably not attack churches in those days, but his attacks against individual Christians will continue and increase. Revelation 12:17 informs us that Satan will make war with all those who "keep the commandments of God and hold to the testimony of Jesus." Satan will also attack Christians through the person of the antichrist (2 Thessalonians 2:9), who will "conquer" God's people (Revelation 13:7) and "prevail" over them (Daniel 7:21).

In the next chapter, I will bring our discussion on Satan's blueprint against Christians to a close, focusing special attention on Satan's promotion of false religions, persecution against God's people, and his efforts to restrict religious freedom.

8

SATAN'S SCHEMES:

False Religions, Persecution, and Reducing Religious Freedom

S atan is a master niche marketer of false ideas in these last days. There's virtually something for everyone in the kingdom of the cults and the various false religions around the world.[1] Satan provides a variety of deceptive options to satisfy people's varied desires.

Inspiring Cults and False Religions

Those who find an appeal in being their own gods might look to the New Age movement or perhaps to Mormonism. If personal empowerment and creating your own reality appeals to you, then (again) the New Age movement might be just right for you. If you like health and wealth, then the Word-Faith movement might be for you. If you dislike pain, suffering, and death, then maybe Christian Science is your ticket—since this cult categorizes pain, suffering, and death as "errors of the mortal mind." If you're more interested in contacting dead loved ones, then perhaps Spiritism is your ticket. If your interest is more on the sensual side, then the Children of God— today called The Family—might be for you, since moral liberty and laxity characterizes this cult. Does living many lives through reincarnation appeal to you? Then maybe you might like Hinduism.

With each cultic group and false religion inspired by Satan, the goal is to keep people away from the true God, the true Jesus, and the true gospel. It is no wonder that Scripture exhorts Christians to beware of Satan's schemes (2 Corinthians 2:11).

"Spirits" have played a major role in the emergence of cults and false religions. Mormonism came from an alleged revelation from the so-called angel Moroni to the "prophet" Joseph Smith. Islam came from alleged revelations from the angel Gabriel to the "prophet" Muhammad.

Swedenborgianism is another example. Emanuel Swedenborg (1688–1772) claimed to be in contact with the spirit world. While in the spirit realm, he claimed he had conversations with many religious luminaries of the past, including the apostle Paul, Augustine, Martin Luther, and John Calvin. These conversations allegedly confirmed his divine calling to derive esoteric (secret and hidden) meanings buried in the text of Scripture. He claimed: "I have written entire pages, and the spirits did not dictate the words, but absolutely guided my hand, so that it was they who were doing the writing."[2]

Yet another example is Theosophy—a forerunner to the New Age movement, headed by Helena Petrovna Blavatsky. She claimed to be in contact with spiritual ascended masters whose alleged goal is to help humanity evolve spiritually.

Likewise, various leaders in the New Age movement have claimed to be in contact with spirit entities from the great beyond.

An example is Kevin Ryerson (Shirley MacLaine's channeler), who claimed to be in contact with various spirits. I have been in the same room with Ryerson, observing him contact these spirit entities, and while he thinks he's in contact with departed humans, in reality I believe he is in contact with demonic spirits. (I do not recommend other Christians attempt this. Only apologists who have studied the cults and the occult should engage in such research— and then only alongside another apologist of equal credentials. In my case, it was the late Elliot Miller, former editor of the *Christian Research Journal.*)

I could give many more examples, but this is enough to illustrate how many cultic groups and false religions have derived from demonic spirits. Such "revelations" from the "other side" are pervasive in our day.

Scripture warns us that Satan can masquerade as an angel of light, seeking to deceive people (2 Corinthians 11:14). First John 4:1 urges believers to "test the spirits." There are lots of false revelations coming from wicked spirit entities today, and we must test these teachings against the Scriptures, which are inspired by the Holy Spirit, the "Spirit of truth" (John 14:17; 15:26; 16:13).

Current statistics prove beyond any doubt that false religions and cults have deceived myriads of people. Islam boasts over 1.8 billion adherents, encompassing over 24 percent of earth's population. Hinduism has 851 million followers and Buddhism has 375 million followers. Meanwhile, the cults used to exist on the outer fringes of our society, but today they've gone mainstream. They're now on TV, on radio, have national magazines, and have PR firms running national and even international advertising campaigns. Each year that passes, increasing numbers of people are being swallowed up in the kingdom of the cults.

What kinds of false doctrines are emerging out of the cults and false religions? Typically, these include:

- *New revelations*—either from God or some other spiritual entity, all of which trump revelations in the Bible.

- *A denial of the sole authority of the Bible*—advocating either new holy books or new revelations from spirit entities.

- *A distorted view of God*—including pantheism (all is God), polytheism (there are many gods), and religious dualism (there is a good god and a bad god).

- *A distorted view of Jesus Christ*—denying His deity, His crucifixion, and His physical resurrection from the dead.

- *A distorted view of Christ's work at the cross*—denying that Christ's death on the cross atoned for humankind's sins.

- *A distorted view of the Holy Spirit*—claiming He is a divine force and not a person in the Trinity.

- *A distorted view of humankind*—claiming that humans are a part of God and hence can create their own realities, or that humans can *become* God.

- *A denial of salvation by grace*—emphasizing that works are necessary for salvation.

The deception being promulgated by false religions and cults is monumental. Today we are witnessing a plethora of false Christs (Matthew 24:24; Mark 13:22), false prophets (Matthew 24:11), and false apostles (2 Corinthians 11:13; Revelation 2:2), all setting forth "teachings of demons" (1 Timothy 4:1).

It grieves me to say it, but I think it will get even worse in the coming years. What is taking place now is setting the stage for the ultimate deceptions that will emerge during the future seven-year tribulation period under the false prophet and the antichrist (see Revelation 13).

Instigating Persecution and Martyrdom

Satan can incite persecution—and even the martyrdom—of Christians worldwide. To the church in Smyrna, the Lord Jesus warned, "Do not fear what you are about to suffer. Behold, the devil is about to throw some of you into prison, that you may be tested, and for ten days you will have tribulation. Be faithful unto death, and I will give you the crown of life" (Revelation 2:10). We are also told that the antichrist—as empowered by Satan (2 Thessalonians 2:9; Revelation 13:2)—will in the tribulation period "make war on the saints" and "conquer them" (Revelation 13:7). Attacking Christians will be a primary tactic of Satan and the antichrist in the end times.

Satan also incites persecution against the Jewish people. In Revelation 12:12-13 we read, "Woe to you, O earth and sea, for the devil has come down to you in great wrath, because he knows that his time is short! And when the dragon saw that he had been thrown down to the earth, he pursued the woman who had given birth to the male child." In context, the "dragon" is Satan, the "woman" is Israel, and the "male child" is Jesus Christ. Satan will persecute Israel—which gave birth to the divine Messiah—during the last half of the tribulation period.

The Scriptures reveal that the persecution and martyrdom of believers will explode during the tribulation period. To clarify, Christians on earth will be raptured prior to the beginning of the tribulation period (1 Thessalonians 1:10; 4:13-17; 5:9; Revelation 3:10). But many people will become believers after the rapture, during the tribulation period (see Matthew 25:31-46; Revelation 7:9-10).

Some may become convinced of the truth of Christianity after witnessing millions of Christians supernaturally vanish off the planet at the rapture. Or perhaps they become believers because of the ministry of the 144,000 Jewish evangelists introduced in Revelation 7 (who themselves come to faith in Christ after the rapture). Perhaps many become believers because of the miraculous ministry of the two witnesses of Revelation 11, prophets who apparently have the same powers as Moses and Elijah. Christian books and videos will also be left behind after the rapture, and many may come to faith because of these.

These converts will become targets for persecution and martyrdom during the tribulation period. Not all will suffer martyrdom, for there will be many still alive at the time of the second coming of Christ (see Matthew 25:31-46). But there will be countless casualties during this seven-year period.

Apparently, there will be significant martyrdom in association with the fifth seal judgment in Revelation 6:9-11:

> When [Jesus] opened the fifth seal, I saw under the altar the souls of those who had been slain for the word of God and for the witness they had borne. They cried out with a loud voice, "O Sovereign Lord, holy and true, how long before you will judge and avenge our blood on those who dwell on the earth?" Then they were each given a white robe and told to rest a little longer, until the number of their fellow servants and their brothers should be complete, who were to be killed as they themselves had been.

This passage reveals that martyrdom will be an ongoing reality during the tribulation period. Some of the martyred "fellow servants" are part of the "great multitude" mentioned in Revelation 7:9-17—"the ones coming out of the great tribulation" who "washed their robes and made them white in the blood of the Lamb" (verse 14).

Revelation 13:7 tells us that the antichrist—energized by Satan—will be the primary instigator of persecution against God's people during the tribulation period. As Daniel 7:21 puts it, the antichrist "made war with the saints and prevailed over them."

These prophecies of persecution and martyrdom relate specifically to the tribulation period, but we are now witnessing initial fulfillments of these prophecies. Just as tremors (or foreshocks) often occur before major earthquakes, so preliminary manifestations of some prophecies emerge prior to the actual tribulation period. Even today we are witnessing the persecution of Christians on a worldwide level. The best current estimates are that 80 percent of all acts of religious persecution around the world today are specifically against Christians.[3]

Moreover, a recent report about a global increase in persecution against Christians informs us, "A horrific catalogue of human rights abuses of Christians and other believers is listed in the latest freedom of religion or belief report from the European Union…It finds 'significant restrictions' exist on religion worldwide, including the near extinction of Christians in Syria and Iraq."[4]

Sobering days lie ahead.

Reducing Religious Freedom

One final tactic of Satan and the antichrist in the end times relates to the deterioration of religious freedom. During the tribulation period, the false religion associated with New Babylon will seek primacy and exclusivity worldwide, and will persecute those who do not submit—especially Christians. Scripture reveals that in New Babylon's streets will flow "the blood of the prophets and of God's holy people and the blood of people slaughtered all over the world" (Revelation 18:24 NLT). This false religion will be "drunk with the blood of the saints, the blood of the martyrs of Jesus" (Revelation 17:6).

Later, after the antichrist and his associates destroy this false religion (Revelation 17:16), the antichrist—who will exalt himself to the level of deity—will seek to be the sole object of worship worldwide. The false prophet—the antichrist's righthand man—will seek to enforce the "mark of the beast": "It causes all, both small and great, both rich and poor, both free and slave, to be marked on the right hand or the forehead, so that no one can buy or sell unless he has the mark" (Revelation 13:16-17).

The global religion associated with New Babylon during the tribulation period will not tolerate competing religions. Likewise, the antichrist—who will claim deity and demand worship—will not tolerate competing religions. This necessitates a reduction in religious tolerance worldwide.

Even now we are witnessing preliminary manifestations of the waning of religious freedom. While Americans still enjoy the constitutional right of freedom of religion, there has been a massive societal shift away from being faith-friendly to Christians and Christianity. In the crosshairs today are Christian holidays, nativity scenes at Christmastime, Christian morality, the Bible, and public displays of the cross. Many today also seek to marginalize Christian influence in schools and education, in government, in public policy, and in the media.

Meanwhile, there remains a strong anti-Christian bias in Hollywood films and television. Christians continue to be demonized in the popular media. A favorite media tactic is to use the pejorative term *religious right* to describe Christian conservatives. The intent is to portray Christians as intolerant backwoods fanatics who do not use their brains—*intellectual Neanderthals*. Humanist secularists are the "enlightened intellectuals" amongst us.

Because of the escalating onslaught, many Christians are feeling the heat regarding their faith. One study reveals:

> When we look at the broadest segment of practicing Christians…a majority says they feel "misunderstood" (54 percent) and "persecuted" (52 percent), while millions of others use terms like "marginalized" (44 percent), "sidelined" (40 percent), "silenced" (38 percent), "afraid to speak up" (31 percent), and "afraid to look stupid" (23 percent) to describe living their faith in society today.[5]

Meanwhile, the religious freedom of Christians around the world has diminished. Among the countries with the greatest religious restrictions against Christians are North Korea, China, Russia, Egypt, Indonesia, Pakistan, and Turkey. In these countries, both the government and society at large have imposed countless limits on the religious beliefs and practices of Christians.

We must also acknowledge the rising threat from Islam. Some Islamic leaders teach that jihad is a foreign policy option that can expand Islamic authority all over the world. Many Shiite Muslims believe that at the apocalyptic end of days, a great, armed jihad will cause the subjugation of the entire world to Islam. Not unexpectedly, attacks on the religious freedom of Christians is heaviest in those Muslim countries with Sharia law:

> The precarious status of churches and other forms of Christian expression under Sharia law is emblematic of

Islam's innate hostility to Christianity. But Islamic law goes further, denying freedom of speech to all Christians and even freedom of conscience and conviction to Christian converts. Sharia curtails these freedoms by means of three laws that, though separate, often overlap: the laws against apostasy, blasphemy, and proselytism. For example, the Muslim who converts to Christianity is guilty of apostasy. But he can also be seen as a blasphemer, whose very existence is an affront to Islam. And when he speaks about Christianity—as enthusiastic new converts often do—around Muslims, he exposes himself to charges of proselytism. These three Islamic laws effectively ban freedom of speech, freedom of religion, and even freedom of thought.[6]

The Bible reveals that religious freedom will steadily wane in the end times. In Matthew 24:9 (NLT) Jesus affirmed, "You will be arrested, persecuted, and killed. You will be hated all over the world because you are my followers." While this verse specifically addresses the tribulation period, we are seeing preliminary manifestations even today, especially in Islamic countries.

Religious oppression even occurs within families. Jesus said, "A brother will betray his brother to death, a father will betray his own child, and children will rebel against their parents and cause them to be killed. And everyone will hate you because you are my followers" (Mark 13:12-13 NLT). Even today we are witnessing "honor killings" in which a father might kill his son or a brother might kill his sister for departing from Islam to become a Christian.

Jesus also warned, "You will be dragged into synagogues and prisons, and you will stand trial before kings and governors because you are my followers" (Luke 21:12 NLT). We are today witnessing this very thing in countries like North Korea, China, Russia, Egypt, Indonesia, Pakistan, and Turkey.

I don't enjoy contemplating it, but the future looks bleak. It is likely that such religious oppression will not only continue but escalate as we draw deeper into the end times.

We need to be mentally and spiritually prepared for this. During these tough days when religious freedom is waning—and persecution and martyrdom of Christians is escalating—Christ is calling His church to a deeper commitment.

Jesus instructed, "If any of you wants to be my follower, you must give up your own way, take up your cross, and follow me" (Mark 8:34 NLT). Jesus is calling for a total commitment. The idea is this: *If you really want to follow Me, do not do so in word only, but put your life on the line and follow Me on the path of the cross—a path that will involve sacrifice, self-denial, and possibly even suffering and death for My sake.*

PART 3

RESISTING AND DEFEATING THE ENEMY

Be strong in the Lord
and in the strength of his might.
Put on the whole armor of God,
that you may be able to stand
against the schemes of the devil.

(EPHESIANS 6:10-11)

9

Our Position in Christ

The single most important component in our victory over the powers of darkness is our position in Christ. As Mark Hitchcock put it, "The best way to keep the enemy out is to keep Christ in. The sheep need not be terrified by the wolf; they have but to stay close to the shepherd."[1]

My friends, the safest place to be when facing spiritual warfare is to be "in Christ." Scripture speaks a great deal about the importance of this, as the following examples show (pay special attention to the italicized words in the verses below):

- We have redemption in Christ. Romans 3:24 says we "are justified by his grace as a gift, through the redemption that is *in Christ Jesus*." Ephesians 1:7 likewise affirms of Christ: "*In him* we have redemption through his blood, the forgiveness of our trespasses, according to the riches of his grace."

- We are dead to sin and alive to God in Christ: "You also

must consider yourselves dead to sin and alive to God *in Christ Jesus*" (Romans 6:11).

- We have eternal life in Christ: "For the wages of sin is death, but the free gift of God is eternal life *in Christ Jesus our Lord*" (Romans 6:23).

- There is no condemnation for those in Christ: "There is therefore now no condemnation for those who are *in Christ Jesus*" (Romans 8:1).

- Nothing can separate us from God's love in Christ: "For I am sure that neither death nor life, nor angels nor rulers, nor things present nor things to come, nor powers, nor height nor depth, nor anything else in all creation, will be able to separate us from the love of God *in Christ Jesus our Lord*" (Romans 8:38-39).

- We have sanctification in Christ: "To the church of God that is in Corinth, to those sanctified *in Christ Jesus*" (1 Corinthians 1:2).

- We have grace in Christ. First Corinthians 1:4 records Paul's words to the church in Corinth: "I give thanks to my God always for you because of the grace of God that was given you *in Christ Jesus*." Likewise, Paul says in 2 Timothy 2:1: "You then, my child, be strengthened by the grace that is *in Christ Jesus*."

- We are triumphant in Christ: "Thanks be to God, who *in Christ* always leads us in triumphal procession" (2 Corinthians 2:14).

- We are new creations in Christ: "Therefore, if anyone is *in Christ*, he is a new creation. The old has passed away; behold, the new has come" (2 Corinthians 5:17).

- We have freedom in Christ. Galatians 2:4-5 speaks of the "freedom that we have *in Christ Jesus*."

- We have every spiritual blessing in Christ: "Blessed be the God and Father of our Lord Jesus Christ, who has blessed us *in Christ* with every spiritual blessing in the heavenly places" (Ephesians 1:3).

- We have the privilege of daily walking in Christ: "Therefore, as you received Christ Jesus the Lord, so walk *in him*" (Colossians 2:6).

- Life is in Christ: "*In him* was life, and the life was the light of men" (John 1:4).

I hope you can see from this brief sampling how important it is for you and me as Christians to live our lives "in Christ." This spiritual reality is truly the secret to victory in spiritual warfare. Mark Bubeck puts it this way:

> The phrases *in the Lord, in Christ,* or their equivalent appear more than forty times in the book of Ephesians alone. Such repetition indicates that such phrases are not convenient clichés. Every Christian is inseparably united with the Lord Jesus Christ. We are placed by God into oneness with Jesus' Person and work. Christ's work belongs to every believer by right of intimate union...Being "in Christ" is a doctrinal fact, an absolute truth that grants to the believer a new stance. The old bondage and fear of Satan has been broken. All of Christ's victory has become ours.[2]

Apart from Bible verses that specifically address our blessings in Christ, other verses provide incredible insights on the importance of our position in Christ.

In John 15:5, Jesus affirmed, "I am the vine; you are the branches. Whoever abides in me and I in him, he it is that bears much fruit, for apart from me you can do nothing." I suggest pairing this verse with Philippians 4:13: "I can do all things through [Christ] who strengthens me."

Can you see how this applies to spiritual warfare? You might look at it this way: *Apart from Christ we can do nothing to attain victory in spiritual warfare, but victory is abundantly ours through Christ who strengthens us.* Never forget that Christ Himself "disarmed the rulers and authorities and put them to open shame, by triumphing over them in him" (Colossians 2:15). So, plug into Christ as a branch plugs into a vine, and Christ's victory becomes your victory.

Another positional truth is found in Romans 8:14-15, where the apostle Paul tells us, "All who are led by the Spirit of God are sons of God…you have received the Spirit of adoption as sons, by whom we cry, 'Abba! Father!'" Because of what Christ has done for you, you've been adopted into God's family. You are God's child (see Galatians 3:26-28; 4:7; Ephesians 1:5). And you are now privileged to call the Father "Abba," which we might loosely paraphrase "Papa."

Think about it: A young child who feels threatened (say, by a barking dog), instinctively calls out to her papa and holds his hand, knowing that she is safe when she is near him. Likewise, the child of God who feels threatened by the powers of darkness can call out to Papa any time, knowing that the closer he or she stays to Him, the safer he or she is. This is part of the blessing you have a result of your position in Christ (see Romans 8:16,31,37).

Yet another positional truth surfaces in Romans 13:14, where we are instructed to "put on the Lord Jesus Christ, and make no provision for the flesh, to gratify its desires." This is important because giving in to fleshly sins can open the door for Satan to work in our lives. To prevent this, David Jeremiah advises that every morning after arising, we ought to "wear Christ like we wear a suit of clothes."[3] Since Christ has already attained victory over the powers of darkness (Colossians 1:13; 2:15; Hebrews 2:14-15), His victory becomes our victory when we wear Him like a suit (see 1 Corinthians 15:57; 6:17; Ephesians 6:10; Revelation 12:11).

Jeremiah's admonition is similar to that of the late Ray Stedman:

> When I get up in the morning, I put on my clothes, intending them to be part of me all day, to go where I go and do what I do. They cover me and make me presentable to others. That is the purpose of clothes. In the same way, the apostle is saying to us, "Put on Jesus Christ when you get up in the morning. Make Him a part of your life that day. Intend that He go with you everywhere you go, and that He acts through you in everything you do. Call upon His resources. Live your life in Christ.[4]

Closely related to this is the positional truth in Galatians 2:20, where the apostle Paul writes, "I have been crucified with Christ. It is no longer I who live, but Christ who lives in me. And the life I now live in the flesh I live by faith in the Son of God, who loved me and gave himself for me." The Amplified Bible renders it this way: "I have been crucified with Christ [that is, in Him I have shared His crucifixion]; it is no longer I who live, but Christ lives in me. The life I now live in the body I live by faith [by adhering to, relying on, and completely trusting] in the Son of God, who loved me and gave Himself up for me."

For Paul, this meant that his sinful and prideful self died along with Christ. Paul thus yielded his life to another—one who never sinned, one who was God incarnate, one who was raised from the dead. Paul was unable to live the Christian life in his own strength, but by virtue of his co-crucifixion with Christ, the resurrected Christ now lived in Paul and gave him the victory. All this happens by faith in Christ.

As it was with Paul, so it is with us. We attain the victory as Christ lives the Christian life through us. His victory becomes our victory. His power becomes our power.

Charles Ryrie gets more specific and tells us that *crucifixion with Christ* and *Christ living in me* means "death to or separation from the reigning power of the old sinful life and freedom to experience the power of the resurrection life of Christ by faith."[5] This truth deals a double deathblow to the powers of darkness: (1) *Death to the reigning power of sin* is important because it nullifies the means demons like to use in finding entry into our lives (sin opens the door for them). (2) *Experiencing the power of the resurrection life of Christ by faith* is important because Christ's victory over the powers of darkness becomes our victory over the powers of darkness. Christ's power becomes our power!

We encounter yet another positional truth in Ephesians 2:13, which affirms, "Now in Christ Jesus you who once were far off have been brought near by the blood of Christ." We understand this verse in terms of the distinction between Jews and Gentiles: "Now in Christ Jesus you who once were far off [that is, you Gentiles, as opposed to us Jews] have been brought near to God by the blood of Christ." My friends, you must *count on* or *reckon on* this as being true in your life. Satan loves to divert your attention to your failures before God, and may even make you feel like you're not a real Christian, and that God is furious with you because of your sins. When that happens, remind yourself—*and count on it as being true*—that you have been "brought near" to God by the blood of Christ alone. Not by your works. Not by your attempted good deeds. Not by church attendance. But by the blood of Christ alone. Because of Christ's death on your behalf, "You are no longer strangers and aliens, but you are fellow citizens with the saints and members of the household of God" (Ephesians 2:19). *You are forever in God's family!*

One of my favorite positional truths is found in Philippians 4:19: "And my God will supply every need of yours according to his riches in glory in Christ Jesus." Have you ever wondered, "Where can I find the strength to be the Christian I know I should be?" "How can I overcome all that faces me this week?" "I'm overwhelmed. How can I possibly survive?" "I've fallen yet again, Lord. I succumbed to the devil's temptation again. (Sigh!)"

Brothers and sisters, God never intended for you to engage in spiritual warfare—let alone face all the difficulties of daily life— relying on your own resources. Christ is infinitely rich in divine resources. Philippians 4:19 tells us we need to plug ourselves into Christ's divine resources and not rely on our own. Only then is victory possible.

There are many other wonderful verses about our blessings in Christ. But I hope you're now beginning to see why Christian leaders across the board have concluded that our only means of victory in spiritual warfare hinges on our position in Christ. Without staying plugged in to Christ in His exalted position, we stand no chance in repelling the forces of darkness.

Consider these words from Christian leaders:

Warren Wiersbe: "You are not fighting FOR victory, but FROM victory, for Jesus Christ has already defeated Satan!"[6]

Kay Arthur: "Christ has already won, and we get to live in His victory. The enemy is dangerous, but Christ is victorious."[7]

Chip Ingram: "Spiritual warfare is never an attempt to gain the victory. It is standing firm in what we already possess…When we fight, we're not trying to win. We're enforcing the victory that Jesus has already secured. In his power, we are invincible."[8]

Tony Evans: "Only when we stand firm under Christ's Word and authority will we be able to live victoriously in spiritual warfare…Until you stand firm under the comprehensive rule of God in your life and in union with your identity in Jesus Christ, you will only find a temporary reprieve. Only in Christ will you find the authority to live in victory."[9]

Merrill Unger: "[The Christian's position in Christ is] an impregnable fortress, which all the hosts of hell cannot break through. God creates that fortress and guards its inviolability by the redemptive work of His Son and the unchangeable truth of His Word."[10]

C. Fred Dickason: "God has given Christ all authority in heaven and on earth (Matthew 28:18; Ephesians 1:20-23; Philippians 2:9-10). The Christian stands in the authority of Christ as his official representative (2 Corinthians 5:20). With such backing, we have nothing to fear." Dickason also affirms that "we ourselves must be subject to Christ's authority (Romans 12:1-2). We must first submit to God, then we can resist the devil in the authority of Christ (James 4:7)."[11]

If all this seems new to you, guess who's been blinding your mind to these glorious truths? That's right. It's Satan. He does not want you to understand all this. Satan does not fear you a bit. But he fears Jesus, the divine Messiah, the Son of God, Immanuel ("God with us"), the Good Shepherd, the King of kings and Lord of lords, the Lamb of God, the light of the world, Redeemer, Savior, the resurrection and the life, and the true vine. Christians who have learned this glorious truth are dangerous to Satan and his cause. Now that you have learned it, only one thing remains: *You must put it into action! Do not delay. Act now.*

I make two final points as I draw this chapter to a close.

First, Hebrews 4:15-16 tells us, "We do not have a high priest who is unable to sympathize with our weaknesses, but one who in every respect has been tempted as we are, yet without sin. Let us then with confidence draw near to the throne of grace, that we may receive mercy and find grace to help in time of need." Christ has "been there, done that," to use modern vernacular. He knows what spiritual warfare is like. He knows what temptations are like. By staying strongly rooted in Him day to day, we will increasingly experience the divine Shepherd's protection against the wicked wolves and their enticements. He knows what you're going through. Trust Him to help you and sustain you through the battle.

Second, it is wisest to keep your eyes *perpetually* focused on the divine Shepherd, not on the wicked wolves. Too many Christians mistakenly do the reverse. I think A.W. Tozer is right when he says:

> The scriptural way to see things is to set the Lord always before us, put Christ in the center of our vision, and if Satan is lurking around he will appear on the margin only and be seen as but a shadow on the edge of the brightness. It is always wrong to reverse this—to set Satan in the focus of our vision and push God out to the margin. Nothing but tragedy can come of such inversion.[12]

Mark Hitchcock puts it into proper perspective:

> We need to remember that in Paul's letters, he uses the word "Satan" only ten times and "devil" only six times. Conversely, we find the words "Jesus" in 219 verses,

"Lord" in 272 verses, and "Christ" in 389 verses. Clearly, we are to rivet our attention on Christ, not Satan. We're to be Christ-centered, not Satan-centered.[13]

Rick Stedman gives us a word picture to help us understand this truth better:

> How do we get rid of the darkness when we go into a dark room late at night?…We turn on the light. It's the same in the supernatural realm. To get rid of the darkness of evil, we turn on the light of Christ. We bring Jesus into the situation, which is to ask him to fill us and, by his very presence, shine the light of glory. Light always conquers darkness. Light always prevails. Focus on Jesus rather than the evil one; it works better and it's safer for your soul.[14]

Of course, this does not contradict our earlier emphasis on becoming aware of Satan's tactics to bring us down. Scripture itself exhorts us to gain knowledge of his many tactics so we'll know what to watch for (2 Corinthians 2:11; Ephesians 6:11). The first step to overcoming your enemy is to *know* your enemy. But now that we know about him and his devious tactics, we overcome his efforts by standing strong in our position in Christ.

It is our position in Christ that brings the devil's tactics down like a house of cards. Keep your eyes on Jesus (Hebrews 12:2)!

10

The Role of the Holy Spirit

Jesus informed the disciples in the Upper Room, "I will ask the Father, and he will give you another Helper, to be with you forever, even the Spirit of truth" (John 14:16-17). The word *helper* is rich—carrying the meaning of "counselor, comforter, advocate, one who strengthens." The concepts of encouragement, support, care, the shouldering of responsibility for another's welfare, and advocating truth are all conveyed by this one word. The Holy Spirit's relevance in spiritual warfare cannot be overstated.

There are two New Testament Greek words that translate into the word *another*. The first means "another of a different kind." The second means "another of the same kind." John 14:16 uses this second word.

Jesus said He would ask the Father to send another Helper *of the same kind* as Himself—that is, a personal, ever-present helper. Just as Jesus was a personal comforter who helped the disciples for three years during His earthly ministry, so also would Christ's followers have another personal comforter—the Holy Spirit—who would be with them throughout their lives.

What a wonderful truth this is! We are never alone in our troubles. We are never alone when we are being attacked by fallen angels. When life seems too much for us—when we encounter tough times or we're treated unfairly or we just sense oppression from the powers of darkness—we can rejoice in the presence of the Holy Spirit who comforts, helps, and encourages us. We always have an advocate by our side.

The Comforter Is a Real Person

Many people—including some Christians—have assumed that the Holy Spirit is God's power or a divine force that emanates from Him. But Scripture portrays the Holy Spirit as a bona fide person. It's important to get this right, because a real person with all the attributes of personality—mind, emotions, and will—can assist you when you encounter spiritual warfare. A person can sympathize with what you're going through with the forces of darkness; a force cannot. A person can comfort you and help you in the midst of the attack; a force cannot. A person can stand by your side against evil; a force cannot.

Let's look at some facts that help us understand the personality of the Holy Spirit.

Attributes of Personality

The three primary attributes of personality are mind, emotions, and will. A power or force does not have these attributes. You and I have these attributes. So does the Holy Spirit.

The Holy Spirit has a mind. The Holy Spirit's intellect is clear in 1 Corinthians 2:10, where we read that "the Spirit searches everything" (see also Isaiah 11:2; Ephesians 1:17). The Greek word for *search* means to "thoroughly investigate." The very next verse

(1 Corinthians 2:11) says the Holy Spirit "comprehends" the thoughts of God. Romans 8:27 tells us that just as the Holy Spirit knows the things of God, so God the Father knows "what is the mind of the Spirit." The Holy Spirit has a mind just like you and I and all other persons. Because the Holy Spirit has a mind, He knows who your spiritual enemy is, and knows just how to be your Helper and Comforter during your spiritual conflict.

The Holy Spirit has emotions. Ephesians 4:30 admonishes us: "Do not grieve the Holy Spirit of God." Grief is an emotion and is not something that a power or a force can experience. The Holy Spirit feels the emotion of grief when believers sin. Such sins might include lying, anger, stealing, laziness, and speaking words that are unkind (verses 25-29). Because the Holy Spirit has emotions, He understands *your* emotions—including the negative emotions that surface when Satan flings his flaming darts at you. That makes Him better equipped to be your Comforter.

The Holy Spirit has a will. The Holy Spirit's will is clear in 1 Corinthians 12:11, where we read that He distributes spiritual gifts "to each one individually as he wills." The phrase "he wills" translates the Greek word *bouletai*, which refers to "decisions of the will after previous deliberation."[1] The Holy Spirit makes a sovereign choice regarding what spiritual gifts each Christian receives. A power or force does not have such a will. Just as Satan wills your downfall, so the Holy Spirit—your Helper and Comforter—wills your victory. And the Holy Spirit is more powerful than Satan (1 John 4:4).

～ The Holy Spirit's Works Confirm His Personality

The Holy Spirit does many things in Scripture that only a person can do. The Holy Spirit teaches others (John 14:26), bears witness to things (John 15:26), guides people (Romans 8:14), commissions people to service (Acts 13:4), issues commands to people (Acts 8:29), prays for believers (Romans 8:26), and speaks to people (John 15:26; 2 Peter 1:21). Let's consider three personal works in a little more detail.

The Holy Spirit bears witness. John 15:26 tells us that the Holy Spirit "will bear witness" of Christ. Bearing witness is something only a person can do. The disciples bore witness about Christ (John 15:27). John the Baptist bore witness to the truth (John 5:33). Likewise, the Holy Spirit bears witness about Christ. The Spirit constantly reminds us that Jesus empowers us for victory over the powers of darkness and that our position in Christ is a key to spiritual victory.

The Holy Spirit prays for believers. Romans 8:26 tells us, "Likewise the Spirit helps us in our weakness. For we do not know what to pray for as we ought, but the Spirit himself intercedes for us with groanings too deep for words." Just as Jesus (a person) intercedes for believers (Romans 8:34; Hebrews 7:25), so the Holy Spirit (a person) intercedes for believers. When I'm experiencing spiritual warfare, it is comforting to know that both Jesus *and* the Holy Spirit are interceding for me! They are both on my side.

The Holy Spirit issues commands. Acts 8:29 tells us that the Holy Spirit directed Philip to speak to the Ethiopian eunuch. Acts 13:2 tells us that the Holy Spirit commanded that Paul and Barnabas engage in missionary work. Acts 13:4 affirms that these two men were "sent out by the Holy Spirit." A power or force cannot command and send individuals to specific places. Only a person can do that.

Other Persons Treat the Holy Spirit as a Person

Other persons consistently treat the Holy Spirit as a person throughout Scripture.

The Father sent the Holy Spirit. Just as Jesus was "sent" by the Father (John 6:38), so also was the Holy Spirit sent by the Father (John 14:26; 16:7). One does not "send" an impersonal power.

One can blaspheme the Holy Spirit. A force (electricity, for example) or a thing (a computer, for example) cannot be on the receiving end of blasphemy. One can, however, blaspheme the Father (Revelation 13:6; 16:9). One can blaspheme the Son (Matthew 27:39; Luke 23:39). In like manner, one can blaspheme the Holy Spirit (Matthew 12:32; Mark 3:29-30). Like the Father and the Son, the Holy Spirit is a holy person.

Some persons lie to the Holy Spirit. Acts 5:3 reveals that Ananias and Sapphira were guilty of lying to the Holy Spirit. A person does not lie to a mere power. Can you imagine how people might respond if I stood up in church one Sunday morning and confessed to lying to the electricity in my home?

Since the Holy Spirit has all the attributes of personality, and since He does things only a person can do, and since other persons treat the Holy Spirit as a person, the only viable conclusion is that the Holy Spirit—the divine Helper and Comforter—is a person.

But Why Doesn't the Holy Spirit Have a Name?

Some people object that because the Holy Spirit does not have a personal name, He cannot truly be a person. This is a weak argument. Spiritual beings do not always possess names in Scripture. An example is how evil spirits remain unnamed throughout Scripture. Scripture designates them "unclean spirits" or "wicked spirits." Their designation reflects their character. The same is true of the Holy Spirit. His designation reflects His character. This makes a name unnecessary.

Besides, notice that Jesus in Matthew 28:19 instructs His

followers, "Go therefore and make disciples of all nations, baptizing them *in the name* of the Father and of the Son and of the Holy Spirit" (italics added). In this verse, the Father, the Son, and the Holy Spirit have the same "name." The Holy Spirit is just as much a person as the Father and the Son. And all three persons help us when we face spiritual warfare.

The Comforter Is God

The Holy Spirit is not only a person, He is also God. He is just as much God as the Father and Jesus are. He is the third person of the Holy Trinity. This is important, for only God's power suffices to bring victory over Satan and the fallen angels. Scripture affirms that "he who is in you is greater than he who is in the world" (1 John 4:4). This means that the Holy Spirit who indwells us is greater than Satan.

How do we know the Holy Spirit is God? Scripture refers to the Holy Spirit as both "God" (Acts 5:3-4) and "Lord" (2 Corinthians 3:17-18). Scripture also identifies Him as Yahweh (Acts 7:51; 28:25-27; 1 Corinthians 2:12; Hebrews 3:7-9; 10:15-17; 2 Peter 1:21) and refers to Him as divine (Matthew 12:32; Mark 3:29; 1 Corinthians 3:16; 6:19; Ephesians 2:22). The Holy Spirit is the "Spirit of God" (Genesis 1:2; Exodus 31:3; Numbers 24:2; Job 33:4; Ezekiel 11:24; Romans 8:9,14; 1 Corinthians 2:11,14; 1 Peter 4:14; 1 John 4:2).

The Holy Spirit also has all the attributes of God. For example, the Holy Spirit is everywhere-present (Psalm 139:7), all-knowing (1 Corinthians 2:10), all-powerful (Romans 15:19), eternal (Hebrews 9:14), and holy (John 16:7-14).

The Holy Spirit performs works that only God can do. For example, the Holy Spirit joined with the Father and the Son in creating the universe (Genesis 1:2; Job 33:4; Psalm 104:30) and He inspired Scripture (2 Timothy 3:16; 2 Peter 1:21). I find it relevant that the

Holy Spirit—as the "Spirit of truth" (John 16:13)—inspired Scripture, for His words are in antithesis to those of Satan, the "father of lies" (John 8:44). Thus our best source of truth in standing against the lies and deceptions of the devil is Scripture.

The Comforter Glorifies Christ

Scripture reveals that a primary purpose of the Holy Spirit is to bring glory to Jesus. When Jesus met with His disciples in the Upper Room, He informed them that the Holy Spirit "will glorify me, for he will take what is mine and declare it to you" (John 16:14). The goal of the Spirit is not to make Himself or His agenda prominent but to magnify and exalt the person and words of Jesus. He seeks to interpret and apply Jesus' teachings to His followers so that Jesus becomes central to their thinking and real in their lives. There's nothing that makes the Holy Spirit happier than for people to fall in love with Jesus and follow Him in all their ways.

We might say that the work of the Holy Spirit among believers is Christocentric—meaning that Christ is the very center of the Spirit's work among believers. Everything He does exalts Christ and glorifies Him.

This ultimately means that the Holy Spirit exalts the very one who defeated the devil. Hebrews 2:14-15 says this of Jesus: "Since therefore the children share in flesh and blood, he himself likewise partook of the same things, that through death he might destroy the one who has the power of death, that is, the devil, and deliver all those who through fear of death were subject to lifelong slavery." Jesus thus "disarmed the rulers and authorities and put them to open shame, by triumphing over them in him" (Colossians 2:15). The more the Holy Spirit exalts Christ in your heart, the more afraid the powers of darkness become!

Ministries of the Holy Spirit

Scripture affirms that the Holy Spirit engages in many wonderful ministries among believers. Let's consider a few of these.

The Holy Spirit seals believers. The apostle Paul informs us that at the moment we believe in Jesus, we are "sealed for the day of redemption" (Ephesians 4:30). Indeed, we are "sealed with the promised Holy Spirit, who is the guarantee of our inheritance" (1:13-14).

In ancient Rome, documents sent from one location to another had a seal imprinted with a Roman stamp. The authority of the Roman government protected that document against unauthorized opening. The seal served as a guarantee that the document would reach its final destination.

In the same way, you and I as believers have the seal of the Holy Spirit. This seal serves as a guarantee that we will reach our final destination—eternal life in heaven. The Holy Spirit, as our seal, represents assurance and security. No one can break God's seal.

I live in Texas. Each spring the cattle ranchers round up all their one-year-old calves for branding. The brand imprints directly on the calf's flank. This is the rancher's mark of ownership. Once the branding process is complete, no one can dispute that the calf belongs to him.

In like manner, God has placed His mark of ownership on us by the seal of the Holy Spirit. We are "branded" for God. No one can remove us from His ownership, and this assures that our destiny in heaven is secure.

Why is this relevant for spiritual warfare? One of Satan's tactics is to get you on such a guilt trip from your failures before God that you doubt your salvation. The devil may whisper to your mind's ear: "You're such a bad sinner that God has kicked you out of His eternal family." Nothing could be further from the truth. You have the seal of the Holy Spirit. You've got God's brand on you. Your salvation is secure! It's a done deal.

The Holy Spirit guides believers. Brothers and sisters, God does not expect us to find our way alone. He does not abandon us to wander around in the darkness trying to find the light. He does not expect us to journey toward the promised land of heaven all by ourselves. The Holy Spirit is ever with us, guiding us along the way. John 16:13 tells us that the Holy Spirit guides us into all truth and reveals the things of Christ to us. The lyrics of a hymn by Marcus Wells beautifully depict this ministry of the Holy Spirit:

> Holy Spirit, faithful Guide,
> Ever near the Christian's side;
> Gently lead us by the hand,
> Pilgrims in a desert land;
> Weary souls fore'er rejoice,
> While they hear that sweetest voice,
> Whisp'ring softly, "Wanderer come!
> Follow Me, I'll guide thee home."

We can sometimes feel lost and directionless, especially when in the throes of spiritual warfare. When we feel that way, the Holy Spirit is always there to take us by the hand and guide us. *We are never alone.*

The Filling of the Holy Spirit

When the apostle Paul instructs us to "be filled with the Spirit" in Ephesians 5:18, he states this as an imperative in the original Greek. This means being filled by the Holy Spirit is not a mere option for the Christian but is a command. "Filled" is also in the present tense in the original Greek, meaning that being filled needs to be continuous and ongoing. Day by day, moment by moment, you and I as Christians are commanded to be filled with the Spirit. But what does this mean?

The context of the verse provides us with the answer. Consider the verse in its entirety: "Do not get drunk on wine, which leads to debauchery. Instead, be filled with the Spirit" (Ephesians 5:18 NIV). Both drunk and Spirit-filled persons are *controlled* persons—that is, they're under the influence of either alcohol or the Spirit, and as a result they do things unnatural to them. In both cases they abandon themselves to an influence.

To be filled with the Holy Spirit means that we will be controlled or governed no longer by self but by the Spirit. It is not a matter of gaining more of the Holy Spirit but rather of the Holy Spirit gaining more control of us.

A believer becomes "filled with the Spirit" when he or she purposefully yields to the indwelling Holy Spirit. This results in a spiritual condition in which the Holy Spirit controls and empowers the individual moment by moment. The person "full of the Holy Spirit" behaves in a way that's consistent with that filling. Put another way, the person acts in a way that's pleasing to God.

Who do you think stands a better chance of victory in spiritual warfare? The person with self in control? Or the person with the Holy Spirit in control? The answer is obvious. Yielding daily to the control of the Holy Spirit is one of the wisest steps a Christian can take in keeping his or her defenses strong in the face of spiritual warfare.

Walking in the Spirit

Ever since Adam and Eve's fall into sin, all people have been born into the world with a sin nature. This sin nature reveals itself through many kinds of fleshly sin—"sexual immorality, impurity, sensuality, idolatry, sorcery, enmity, strife, jealousy, fits of anger, rivalries, dissensions, divisions, envy, drunkenness, orgies, and things like these" (Galatians 5:19-21). In our own strength, we do not have the power to resist such evil inclinations of our sin nature. But we can have victory over the sin nature by walking in dependence upon the Holy Spirit. Galatians 5:16 tells us, "Walk by the Spirit, and you will not gratify the desires of the flesh."

In this verse, *walk* is a present-tense verb. This shows continuous action. We are to persistently and continually walk in dependence upon the Holy Spirit. When we do this, we live in a way that is pleasing to God. Walking in dependence upon the Spirit enables us to overcome all the fleshly sins listed above.

Can you see the relevance of this for spiritual warfare? Fleshly sins can be entry points for the powers of darkness in your life. The enemy might even gain a stronghold in your life through one of these sins if you are persistent in it and do not repent. By walking in dependence on the Holy Spirit, however, you not only avoid such sins, but short circuit demonic attempts to gain entry into your life. It is therefore in your best interests to daily walk in dependence on the Holy Spirit.

The Fruit of the Spirit

As we walk in dependence upon the Spirit, not only do we enjoy victory over fleshly sins, we also find the fruit of the Spirit cropping up in our lives. Galatians 5:22-23 tells us that "the fruit of the Spirit is love, joy, peace, patience, kindness, goodness, faithfulness, gentleness, [and] self-control."

Theologians often note that as we look at the qualities listed in Galatians 5:22-23, we find an accurate profile of Jesus Christ. We might say that walking in the Spirit reproduces the character of the

Lord in our lives. In this way, we progressively take on the family likeness as members of God's family.

I once read a story about a slothful man who moved into a new house. The house quickly began to show the effects of his untidy lifestyle. The yard became littered with trash. The lawn withered for lack of care. The house became cluttered.

Later, a young family bought the house and moved in. They painted the house, cleaned the yard, and replanted the lawn. There was a dramatic improvement in that house because there was a change in occupants.

That's ultimately the way it is with a person who becomes a Christian and walks in dependence upon the Holy Spirit. There is a dramatic change in that person's life because there is a perfect, new resident within—the Holy Spirit. And as we walk in dependence upon the Spirit, His fruit grows in our lives.

I'm sure you can see the relevance of the fruit of the Holy Spirit for spiritual warfare. Instead of giving place to the devil through anger, our lives are now brimming with love and patience. Instead of giving place to the devil through sexual sin, our lives are now brimming with self-control. Instead of succumbing to discouragement and depression (two of the devil's favorite tactics against us), our lives are now brimming with joy and peace. Walking in dependence on the Holy Spirit, with His subsequent fruit in our lives, has a sledgehammer effect on the tactics of the devil.

Do Not Grieve the Holy Spirit

All this brings me to stress the apostle Paul's sober warning in Ephesians 4:30: "Do not grieve the Holy Spirit of God." In the original Greek text, this verse reads literally: "Stop grieving the Holy Spirit."

Is there a sin in your life that you fall into consistently? If so,

Scripture exhorts you to stop grieving the Holy Spirit with that sin. Choose instead to walk in dependence upon the Holy Spirit. If you meet that condition, you will enjoy victory over the sin.

When the Spirit of God suffers grief within a believer because of sin, the believer becomes vulnerable. Such a state of sin—if there is no repentance—hinders the fellowship, guidance, instruction, and power of the Spirit that make victory in spiritual warfare possible. Though the Holy Spirit continues to indwell the believer, He is not free to accomplish His work. To grieve the Holy Spirit is to say goodbye to the fruit of the Spirit, such as love, joy, peace, and self-control. If these qualities are missing in your life, you become vulnerable to deeper sin and deeper bondage to the powers of darkness.

Complete obedience to God is thus a nonnegotiable requirement for victory in spiritual warfare. Partial obedience will not do. One foot in the kingdom and one foot in the world will not do. Compromise is always a slippery slope leading to defeat. Choose obedience and live as a victor.

11

The Armor of God

Gog has provided us with spiritual armor for our defense in spiritual warfare (Ephesians 6:10-18). Each piece of armor is important and serves its own special purpose. But you and I must put on this armor. God does not force us to dress in it. We do it by choice.

Without wearing this spiritual armor, you and I don't stand a chance against the forces of darkness. But with the armor on, victory is ours. "Wearing" this armor means that such things as righteousness, obedience to the will of God, faith in God, guarding our thought lives, God's peace guarding our hearts, and an effective use of the Word of God will daily characterize our lives. These are what spell D-E-F-E-A-T for the devil. In effect, putting on the armor of God amounts to putting on Jesus Christ, who Himself defeated the devil (Matthew 4:3-11; Acts 10:38). Let's consider some details.

Be Strong in the Lord

Ephesians 6:10 begins with an exhortation to "be strong in the Lord and in the strength of his might." The Amplified Bible renders this, "Be strong in the Lord [draw your strength from Him and be empowered through your union with Him] and in the power of His [boundless] might."

"Be strong" is in the present tense in the original Greek, indicating continuous action. We might reword the Amplified rendering this way: "*Keep on* being strong in the Lord [*keep on* drawing your strength from Him and *keep on* being empowered through your union with Him] and in the power of His [boundless] might." A continuous infusion of strength from the Lord is important, for one never knows precisely when the devil may strike.

The Nature of the Warfare

After instructing us to "be strong in the Lord and in the strength of his might," Paul fills us in on why it's critically important that we "put on" the spiritual armor of God:

> Put on the whole armor of God, that you may be able to stand against the schemes of the devil. For we do not wrestle against flesh and blood, but against the rulers, against the authorities, against the cosmic powers over this present darkness, against the spiritual forces of evil in the heavenly places. Therefore take up the whole armor of God, that you may be able to withstand in the evil day, and having done all, to stand firm (Ephesians 6:11-13).

We learn some important lessons from this passage.

Dressing in just one or two pieces of armor is insufficient. We are to put on the "whole armor of God" (verse 11). It's the whole package taken together that defeats the devil's schemes against us.

The purpose of the armor is that we may "be able to stand against the schemes of the devil" (verse 11). Success in defeating the devil's schemes requires that we meet the conditions. The primary condition entails putting on the "whole armor of God." We can't expect victory if we ignore the conditions.

Our enemies are not physical beings but spiritual beings. They are not "flesh and blood" but fallen angels organized by rank: the rulers, the authorities, the cosmic powers over this present darkness, and the spiritual forces of evil in the heavenly places (verse 12). All ranks of fallen angels submit to Satan's leadership.

When someone says something once, it may or may not be important. When someone says something twice, it is unquestionably important. Paul says for the second time, "Take up the whole armor of God" (verse 13). He does not want his readers to miss this or ignore it. It's as if he is saying, "Everything hinges on this: Be sure to put on the whole armor of God, every single piece." Only then will Christians "be able to withstand in the evil day" and "stand firm" (verse 13).

Following this introduction, Paul zeroes in on the specific pieces of God's armor. We learn something important from each one.

The Belt of Truth

Paul urges, "Stand therefore, having fastened on the belt of truth" (Ephesians 6:14). The belt is a strategic part of a warrior's armor, for it holds together the rest of the armor. That means the belt is foundational to success. In spiritual warfare, the foundation to success is truth. We must know the truth of Scripture, written by the God of truth, for only by that truth can we answer the lies and deceptions of Satan. It is good to remember that...

- Scripture is "the word of truth" (2 Timothy 2:15).
- The Holy Spirit, who inspired Scripture, is the "Spirit of truth" (John 16:13).

- Jesus—the central focus in Scripture—is "the way, and the truth, and the life" (John 14:6).

David Jeremiah, in his *Spiritual Warfare Answer Book*, cites a biography of Winston Churchill (*The Last Lion*) that affirmed that Churchill "adopted, as a working thesis, the assumption that any given foreign policy statement by Hitler was the exact opposite of truth." Jeremiah reflects, "It was an assumption that served Churchill well, for Hitler was a liar and a deceiver from the beginning. We can make the same assumption about the devil."[1] Scripture tells us the devil "does not stand in the truth, because there is no truth in him. When he lies, he speaks out of his own character, for he is a liar and the father of lies" (John 8:44). This is one reason we need to saturate our minds with the truth of Scripture. The more truth we know, the better able we are to be victors in spiritual warfare.

For the Christian, it is not enough to *know* the truth. We must also *live* the truth. We must accept the truth *internally* and then act upon the truth *externally*. That means no hypocrisy. No winking at sin. No compromises. No dishonesty. No unrepentant sin. Part of wearing the "belt of truth" involves living our lives according to that truth.

How do we put on the belt of truth? In addition to learning the truth of Scripture and living according to it, Tony Evans suggests the following prayer:

> Dear Lord, You remind me, "But when He, the Spirit of truth, comes, He will guide you into all the truth" [John 16:13]. So many voices and perspectives surround me—coming from friends, the media, or even my own thoughts—that seek to compete with or counter Your

truth. I realize that my history and the things I have experienced may sometimes cloud what I believe to be true. Please let Your Holy Spirit guide me each and every day into all truth. Guide my thoughts and my decisions. Reveal to me where I am thinking wrong. Correct me where I have gotten off track. And grant me the grace to apply the truth You show me through the Spirit to my words and actions so that I reflect Your image more fully in all I do. In Christ's name, amen.[2]

The Breastplate of Righteousness

Another key component of God's armor is the "breastplate of righteousness" (Ephesians 6:14). Christian leaders differ over what this may mean. Some believe it means that the Christian must engage in righteous behavior to stand against the devil's schemes. Others think the breastplate refers to the positional righteousness every Christian has "in Christ." I think the latter view is correct.

Positional righteousness relates to the doctrine of justification. Negatively, the word *justification* means that at the moment of salvation, one is definitively pronounced not guilty before God. Positively, the word means that one is definitively pronounced righteous before God. At the moment of salvation, Christ's own righteousness imputes to the believer's life. So, from the moment a person places faith in Christ, God sees that person through the lens of Christ's righteousness. It can't get better than that!

If I look through a piece of red glass, everything appears red. If I look through a piece of blue glass, everything appears blue. If I look through a piece of yellow glass, everything appears yellow. Likewise, when we believe in Jesus as our Savior, God looks at us through the "lens" of Jesus. He sees us in all the white holiness of His Son. Our sins are imputed to the account of Christ, and Christ's own righteousness is imputed to our account (Romans 5:18-19). Because of what Christ has done for us, God views us as "pure in heart."

This is an important truth, for Satan—"the accuser" (Revelation 12:10)—constantly attacks us by reminding us of all our sins. When that happens, we must stand our ground on the doctrinal promise that Christ's own righteousness is ours. We must rest our case entirely on the finished work of Jesus Christ, counting on the fact that we are "accepted in the beloved" (Ephesians 1:6 KJV).

I love Martin Luther's well-known prayer: "Lord Jesus, you are my righteousness, I am your sin. You have taken upon yourself what is mine and given me what is yours." There has been a great exchange. Jesus took upon Himself our sins at the cross of Calvary, and in exchange He has given us His righteousness (2 Corinthians 5:21). When the Father looks upon us, He sees us in the white righteousness of His Son. That's the breastplate of righteousness.

Shoes of the Gospel of Peace

The next component of God's armor is shoes of the "gospel of peace" (Ephesians 6:15). A soldier with bad shoes does not fight very well. Such a soldier can easily lose his footing. "How you stand pretty well determines how you will fight. If a fighter loses his footing, he may lose the battle."[3] The same is true of a Christian soldier amid spiritual warfare. The solid footing for the Christian soldier hinges on the "gospel of peace."

Jesus said, "Let not your hearts be troubled" (John 14:1). Paul said, "Do not be anxious about anything" (Philippians 4:6). We can have perfect peace with God and perfect peace in our circumstances through Jesus Christ our Lord.

Scripture often speaks of the divine peace each of us can have:

You keep him in perfect peace whose mind is stayed on you, because he trusts in you (Isaiah 26:3).

Let the peace of Christ rule in your hearts (Colossians 3:15).

Do not be anxious about anything, but in everything by prayer and supplication with thanksgiving let your requests be made known to God. And the peace of God, which surpasses all understanding, will guard your hearts and your minds in Christ Jesus (Philippians 4:6-7).

Jesus said: "Peace I leave with you; my peace I give to you. Not as the world gives do I give to you" (John 14:27).

In Christ Jesus you who once were far off have been brought near by the blood of Christ. For he himself is our peace (Ephesians 2:13-14).

God's divine peace is like a guard over our hearts and our minds. His peace cradles us in an often-hostile world. It is a peace that settles us when things go wrong and gives us tranquility amid the storms of life. It is a peace that provides us hope when life throws us a punch. It is a peace that removes panic when Satan and his fallen angels move against us. Never go into spiritual battle without this peace!

We can put on the shoes of peace by praying a prayer based on the verses we just looked at. It might go something like this:

I thank You, Lord, that I can have perfect peace as I keep my mind stayed upon You. I ask that the peace of Christ will now rule in my heart. I release my anxieties and turn all burdens over to You in prayer, trusting that Your peace—which surpasses all understanding—will now guard my heart and mind. I thank You for this. In Jesus' name, amen.

The Shield of Faith

There are all kinds of flaming darts the devil may fling. You might find yourself targeted at various times with darts of discouragement, doubts, jealousy, covetousness, worry, disappointment, debilitating guilt, or lust. Whatever dart the devil uses, his goal is to disable and incapacitate you as a Christian.

Because of the inherent danger of such darts, we must "take up the shield of faith, with which you can extinguish all the flaming darts of the evil one" (Ephesians 6:16). The "shield of faith" amounts to daily trust in the Lord, no matter what the circumstances. Proper use of the shield of faith enables Christians to maintain their composure during a spiritual assault. Without the shield of faith, those flaming darts will lodge in us and they will hurt!

I believe the energizing force of the shield of faith is the Word of God, brimming with God's promises to help in time of need. The greater the knowledge we have of God's Word, the stronger our shield of faith will be. Conversely, the lesser the knowledge we have of God's Word, the weaker our shield will be.

Christians must become skilled in using this shield, for those flaming darts can do increasingly greater damage unless stopped and neutralized by the shield. You might think about it this way: The flames on a fiery dart are minimal, but if not stopped by the shield of faith, the flames can grow and spread and wreak increased havoc on one's inner being. So, quench those darts immediately. Anchor yourself on the promises of God by faith and look to Jesus—"the founder and perfecter of our faith" (Hebrews 12:2).

The Helmet of Salvation

The next piece of God's armor is the "helmet of salvation" (Ephesians 6:17). A helmet is protective gear worn specifically to protect the head. The helmet of salvation protects the believer's mind from Satan's attacks.

Satan's primary tactic is to target our minds. He wants to influence our thoughts. He knows that our thoughts will determine our behavior. In view of this, the apostle Paul admonishes, "We destroy arguments and every lofty opinion raised against the knowledge of God, and take every thought captive to obey Christ" (2 Corinthians 10:5). This is not a onetime event. It is a continual process. Every moment of every day, we must keep our thoughts on the right track, in submission to God, in resistance to the devil. It is not enough to resist *wrong* thinking (or *Satan-inspired* thinking); we must also pursue *right* thinking (or *God-inspired* thinking).

This again points to the importance of God's Word. We must renew our minds daily from God's Word (Romans 12:2). Our minds need to be saturated with spiritually nourishing truths from God's Word, not damaging lies from the evil world system (1 John 2:15-17). Only the truth of God's Word suffices to repel the lies and deceptions of the evil one.

One of the devil's oft-used lies is, "Maybe you're not a real Christian. Maybe you don't possess salvation." Such doubts can be debilitating. Part of wearing the helmet "of salvation" involves driving the stake into the ground once for all that *you are a Christian and salvation is yours.* Anchor yourself on the promises of God (2 Corinthians 5:21; Ephesians 2:8-9). Take God at His Word.

The Sword of the Spirit / The Word of God

Speaking of the Word of God, Paul's description of God's armor next mentions "the sword of the Spirit, which is the word of God" (Ephesians 6:17). We recall that Jesus used God's Word to defeat the devil during His wilderness temptations (Matthew 4). You and I must learn to do the same.

To be effective in wielding the sword of the Spirit, we must first know the Word of God. Ray Stedman advises us, "Obviously, the greater exposure there is to Scripture the more the Spirit can use this mighty sword in our lives. If you never read or study your Bible, you are vulnerable to defeat and despair. You have no defense; you have nothing to put up against these forces. Therefore, learn to read your Bible regularly."[4]

We do ourselves a huge favor by daily feeding upon the Word of God. More than that, we would be wise to meditate upon Scripture. In Christian meditation, the believer objectively contemplates and deeply reflects upon God's Word (Joshua 1:8; Psalm 1:2; 19:14) and His person and faithfulness (Psalm 119; see also 19:14; 48:9; 77:12; 104:34; 143:5).

The Hebrew word for *meditate* means "murmur." It pictures an individual reading and concentrating so intently on what he's reading in Scripture that his lips move as he reads. Such Christian meditation fills our minds with godly wisdom and insight. Scripture affirms, "Blessed is the man" whose "delight is in the law of the Lord, and on his law he meditates day and night" (Psalm 1:1-2).

It is also wise to memorize God's Word. In Psalm 119:11, the psalmist affirms, "I have stored up your word in my heart, that I might not sin against you." Psalm 37:31 says that God's Word is in the righteous man's heart. In Psalm 40:8, the psalmist states, "I delight to do your will, O my God; your law is within my heart." The benefit to memorizing Scripture is that it provides the Holy Spirit with a large arsenal of truth to use as a sword of the Spirit when attacked by the powers of darkness. The more Scripture we memorize, the more ammo the Holy Spirit has to pull out the exact swords we need to defeat the enemy in the moment of attack.

You might try praying this way as you start out your mornings:

> Dear Lord, I seek to use the Word of God—the sword of the Spirit—effectively as I go about my day. Please align my thoughts, my words, and my actions to Your Word. And when attacked by the devil, enable me to use Your Word to thwart the attack. Guide me to find a correlating truth in the pages of Scripture that I can use to thwart the specific temptation or attack from the devil. I pray in Jesus' name. Amen.

Christ Himself Embodies God's Armor

Many students of God's Word have noticed that Jesus virtually embodies God's armor as described in Ephesians 6:11-18. He is the ultimate fulfillment of each piece of armor. For example:

The belt of truth: Jesus Himself is "the way, and the truth, and the life" (John 14:6).

The breastplate of righteousness: "For our sake he made him to be sin who knew no sin, so that in him we might become the righteousness of God" (2 Corinthians 5:21).

The shoes of the gospel of peace: "Therefore, since we have been justified by faith, we have peace with God through our Lord Jesus Christ" (Romans 5:1).

The shield of faith: We look "to Jesus, the founder and perfecter of our faith" (Hebrews 12:2).

The helmet of salvation: "There is salvation in no one else, for there is no other name under heaven given among men by which we must be saved" (Acts 4:12).

The sword of the Spirit: "In the beginning was the Word, and the Word was with God, and the Word was God. He was in the beginning with God…And the Word became flesh and dwelt among us, and we have seen his glory, glory as of the only Son from the Father, full of grace and truth…No one has ever seen God; the only God, who is at the Father's side, he has made him known" (John 1:1-2,14,18).

If you cannot remember each piece of armor you need to put on, just remember Jesus, who embodies all the armor. Rick Stedman says:

> The way we defeat evil and darkness is by focusing on Jesus. After all, what is the armor of God except the very qualities of Jesus Himself? He is Truth, Righteousness, Peace, the Word, and so on. As followers of Christ, we fight best by clothing ourselves with the very character and person of Christ, and then by allowing the light of Jesus to shine in and through us.[5]

We ought always to keep Jesus as our primary focus in life. Satan and his fallen angels can remain on the periphery of our spiritual vision. The sheep's primary safety from vicious wolves is in staying close to the Shepherd and keeping their eyes focused on Him.

Pray at All times

Paul's description of God's armor ends in Ephesians 6:18 with these words: "praying at all times in the Spirit, with all prayer and supplication. To that end, keep alert with all perseverance, making supplication for all the saints." Prayer is so important in spiritual warfare that I devote the entire next chapter to it.

12

The Role of Prayer

After telling us all about God's armor in Ephesians 6:11-17, Paul says we all ought to be about the business of "praying at all times in the Spirit, with all prayer and supplication. To that end, keep alert with all perseverance, making supplication for all the saints" (verse 18). Prayer is not a piece of the armor, but—as one Bible expositor put it—it is "the atmosphere in which the soldier must live and breathe."[1] Let's take a few moments to unpack this pivotal verse.

Paul speaks of "praying at all times." Elsewhere he said we should "be constant in prayer" (Romans 12:12) and to "pray without ceasing" (1 Thessalonians 5:17). Prayer needs to be continuous and habitual, not sporadic.

How can we pray at all times? We can pray every time a new circumstance calls for it. Small prayers can be our habitual response to new developments throughout our day.

Prayer also needs to be "in the Spirit" (Ephesians 6:18). Rote prayers without a heart commitment are insufficient for the battle in spiritual warfare. Prayers must be "in the Spirit" in the sense that we depend upon guidance from the Holy Spirit in prayer.

There may be times when we feel unable to pray. In such a situation, Romans 8:26 assures us, "The Spirit helps us in our weakness. For we do not know what to pray for as we ought, but the Spirit himself intercedes for us with groanings too deep for words."

Paul urges us to "keep alert" as we pray (Ephesians 6:18). This is as it should be with any good soldier. No soldier who wants to survive allows his attention to lapse when the enemy is near. "We must watch against drowsiness, mind-wandering, and preoccupation with other things. Prayer requires spiritual keenness, alertness, and concentration."[2]

Each of us should also pray "with all perseverance" (Ephesians 6:18). This reminds us of Jesus' instructions on prayer in Matthew 7:7-8: "Ask, and it will be given to you; seek, and you will find; knock, and it will be opened to you. For everyone who asks receives, and the one who seeks finds, and to the one who knocks it will be opened." The tenses in the original Greek for this passage carry the idea, "*Keep on* asking and it will be given; *keep on* seeking and you will find; *keep on* knocking and the door will be opened." This verse explicitly tells us not to give up in prayer. We need to hang in there. That's what is meant by perseverance in prayer.

Paul closes his instruction on prayer in Ephesians 6:18 by urging us to make "supplication for all the saints." Our fellow brothers and sisters in Christ are engaged in spiritual warfare, just as we are. We must therefore support our fellow soldiers by prayer since all of them are targets of Satan. Jesus set an example of how to pray for others in His prayer for Peter: "Simon, Simon, behold, Satan demanded to have you, that he might sift you like wheat, *but I have prayed for you that your faith may not fail*" (Luke 22:31-32, italics added). We should pray for each other that we will maintain a strong faith in the face of demonic adversity.

I find it comforting that the New Testament twice tells us that the Lord Jesus lives in heaven to make intercession for us (Romans 8:34; Hebrews 7:25). He prays for us regularly. I believe His intercession for us includes praying for safety from Satan. He interceded this way for His disciples in John 17:15: "I do not ask that you take them out of the world, but that you keep them from the evil one."

Key Components of Prayer

Aside from Ephesians 6:18, Scripture provides us with many other insights on prayer that can help us in our engagements with the powers of darkness. Scripture affirms that prayer is not just asking for things from God. Prayer also involves thanksgiving, praise, worship, and confession.

Thanksgiving. In prayer we should be "giving thanks always and for everything to God the Father in the name of our Lord Jesus Christ" (Ephesians 5:20; see also Colossians 3:15). We should "enter his gates with thanksgiving" (Psalm 100:4; see also Psalm 95:2). This is important, for Satan does not want us to be thankful to God. He'd be much happier if we were angry at God, as he is. Thanking God shows our trust in Him and our confidence that He is guiding our circumstances for our highest good. So thank Him daily!

Praise. Like David of old, praise for God should be a continuous feature of our prayer lives:

> I will bless the LORD at all times;
> his praise shall continually be in my mouth
> (Psalm 34:1).

Bless the LORD, O my soul,
  and all that is within me,
  bless his holy name!
Bless the LORD, O my soul,
  and forget not all his benefits
                    (Psalm 103:1-2).

We ought to continually "offer up a sacrifice of praise to God" (Hebrews 13:15). We can even "praise the name of God with a song" (Psalm 69:30). Just as Satan hates it when you are thankful to God, so he hates it when you praise God. In fact, when you feel as if the powers of darkness are assaulting you on every side, one of the wisest things you can do is to just start praising God out loud for everything you can think of. I promise you—that is not an environment the powers of darkness feel comfortable in. This strategy has helped me many, many times.

Worship. We should also bow down in worship before the Lord:

Oh come, let us worship and bow down;
  let us kneel before the LORD, our Maker!
                    (Psalm 95:6).

We ought to "worship him who made heaven and earth, the sea and the springs of water" (Revelation 14:7). We should worship Him "with reverence and awe" (Hebrews 12:28) and worship Him alone (Exodus 20:3-5; Deuteronomy 5:7). Satan does not want people to worship God. He wants people to worship him (Matthew 4:9; compare with Revelation 13:4). Audible worship of God is not a comfortable environment for Satan and the fallen angels. Not only that, worshipping God keeps us powerfully God-focused, which is exactly what we want when we're facing spiritual warfare. So, worship God often!

Confession. Confession in prayer is wise, for "whoever conceals his transgressions will not prosper, but he who confesses and forsakes them will obtain mercy" (Proverbs 28:13; see also Psalm 32:5). Scripture promises that "if we confess our sins, he is faithful and just to forgive us our sins and to cleanse us from all unrighteousness" (1 John 1:9). This is critically important because Satan likes to use your sins to build a wedge between you and God. Your sin also opens the opportunity for Satan to work in your life. Your best strategy is to keep short accounts with God by confessing sin as soon as possible.

Requests. Scripture assures us we can also go to God for specific requests. The Lord's Prayer shows that we can pray that God will provide our daily food (Matthew 6:11). The apostle Paul wrote, "Do not be anxious about anything, but in everything by prayer and supplication with thanksgiving let your requests be made known to God. And the peace of God, which surpasses all understanding, will guard your hearts and your minds in Christ Jesus" (Philippians 4:6-7). Among the many things we can specifically ask of God in prayer is this: "Rescue us from the evil one" (Matthew 6:13 NLT).

Seven Principles of Prayer

Aside from the insights on prayer we've just examined, there are seven specific principles of prayer that I have always found helpful:

1. All our prayers are subject to God's sovereign will. If we ask for something God does not want us to have, He will sovereignly deny that request. First John 5:14 instructs us: "This is the confidence that we have toward him, that if we ask anything according to his will he hears us." We know it's God's sovereign will for us to pray for overcoming the evil one, for we find that very request in the Lord's Prayer (see Matthew 6:13).

2. Sin is a big hindrance to prayer being answered. Psalm 66:18 says, "If I had cherished iniquity in my heart, the Lord would not have listened." Isaiah 59:2 warns: "Your sins have hidden his face from you so that he does not hear." This is doubly bad, since sin not only blocks our prayers to God, it also gives an opportunity to the devil to work in our lives.

3. Conversely, living righteously is a great benefit to prayer being answered. Proverbs 15:29 says, "The LORD is far from the wicked, but he hears the prayer of the righteous." John 9:31 urges, "If anyone is a worshiper of God and does his will, God listens to him." This is doubly good, for God not only hears the prayers of the righteous, but that same righteousness removes opportunities from the devil to work in our lives.

4. Pray in faith. Jesus promises, "Have faith in God. Truly, I say to you, whoever says to this mountain, 'Be taken up and thrown into the sea,' and does not doubt in his heart, but believes that what he says will come to pass, it will be done for him. Therefore I tell you, whatever you ask in prayer, believe that you have received it, and it will be yours" (Mark 11:22-24). Beware that Satan wants to undermine your faith with flaming darts of doubt. Don't let him succeed. Keep your shield of faith up.

5. Pray in Jesus' name. Jesus promises, "Whatever you ask in my name, this I will do, that the Father may be glorified in the Son. If you ask me anything in my name, I will do it" (John 14:13-14). Jesus is the bridge between humanity and God the Father (1 Timothy 2:5), and He Himself defeated the devil (Hebrews 2:14).

6. If your prayers seem unanswered, keep trusting God no matter what. Your prayer may have ignited some spiritual warfare behind the scenes you know nothing about (see Daniel 10:13-14). An answer will come soon enough, under God's providence.

7. Beware of distractions. Satan does not want you to pray. He will therefore do anything he can to distract you away from prayer. Whether through discouragement, delays, or disappointments, Satan will attempt to shift your attention to other things. "The reason why prayer often seems difficult to us is because Satan seeks to direct us away from it. He knows how important it is. He will use every possible avenue to keep you from seriously communicating with God because he knows what prayer does—it activates heaven's response on your behalf in accordance with the will of God."[3]

The Benefits of Prayer

It is always in our best interests to pray daily to God. After all, prayer has many benefits:

- Prayer can bring enlightenment about God's purposes for us (Ephesians 1:18-19). This includes enlightenment regarding why we suffer and why God allows us to experience spiritual warfare.

- Prayer can help us understand God's will (Colossians 1:9-12). This is important, for Satan will try to confuse you regarding God's will (see Genesis 3:1,4).

- Prayer can increase our love for other people (1 Thessalonians 3:10-13). This is relevant, for such love can replace the anger that can give a place to the devil to work in your life (Ephesians 4:26).

- Prayer can bring encouragement and strength (2 Thessalonians 2:16-17). This is relevant, because among the flaming darts of Satan are darts of discouragement, depression, and worry (Ephesians 6:16).

- Prayer can help deliver righteous Christians from their troubles (Psalm 34:15-22). This includes troubles relating to spiritual warfare.

- Prayer can keep us from succumbing to lies and falsehood (Proverbs 30:7-9). Such prayer is important so we do not fall for the deceptions of the "father of lies" (John 8:44).

- Prayer can help us live righteously (1 Thessalonians 5:23). This is relevant, for Satan wants you to sin, giving an opportunity for him to work in your life.

- Prayer can bring about healing (James 5:14-15). This is also relevant, since Satan and demons can inflict a variety of bodily ailments (Matthew 4:24; Mark 1:32; Luke 7:21; 9:1; Acts 5:16).

Putting on God's Armor through Prayer

We can put on God's armor through prayer. I invite you to use the following prayer as a starting place for a more extended prayer time each day:

> Dear heavenly Father, it is an awesome privilege to come into Your presence. I enter Your gates with thanksgiving, not only for Your many blessings in my life but also for the spiritual armor You provide to protect me against the assaults from wicked spirits.
>
> I put on this armor by faith, beginning with the belt of truth. I am awed that Scripture is "the word of truth" (2 Timothy 2:15) that is inspired by the Holy Spirit, the "Spirit of truth" (John 16:13)—and that Scripture centers on Jesus Christ, "the way, and the truth, and the life"

(John 14:6). Thank You, Father, that Your truth anchors my life. Thank You also that Satan cannot stand against Your truth. I ask that Your truth empower me and motivate me this day to live the way You want me to. Please also help me to discern any ways I am being deceived by the wicked one.

By faith, I put on the breastplate of righteousness. Thank You for the imputed righteousness that is mine by faith in Jesus Christ (Romans 3:10-20). I praise You, Jesus, for taking what is mine—my sin—so You could give me what is Yours—Your righteousness (2 Corinthians 5:21). I embrace that righteousness at this moment. I thank You that Satan and his fallen angels must retreat before Your righteousness.

By faith, I put on the shoes of peace, knowing that my peace with You rests entirely on my faith in Jesus, who died for me on the cross (Romans 5:1). Please also grant me the emotional peace that passes understanding that comes from transferring all my burdens onto Your all-powerful shoulders (Philippians 4:7).

I also take up the shield of faith. May this shield today block all the flaming darts of the evil one—including the soul-crushing darts of depression, discouragement, worry, and guilt. I have faith, Lord, that You are my ultimate shield (Psalm 28:7; 33:20; 119:114; Proverbs 30:5).

By faith, I put on the helmet of salvation. Please protect my mind from intrusive thoughts intended to distract me from following You and trusting You. Please grant that every thought in my mind will be taken captive to obey Christ and His Word (2 Corinthians 10:5). I pray especially that You protect my mind from doubts about You, Your Word, and my relationship with You.

By faith, I take up the sword of the Spirit, which is the Word of God. Today I live in obedience to Your Word (Psalm 119). Today I use the truth of Your Word to defend myself against the lies and deceptions of the devil (Ephesians 6:17). Today I submit my mind for molding by the truths of Your Word. I reject the deceptions of the devil and the evil world system (Romans 12:2).

Father, by faith I have put on the armor. May this be a day of spiritual victory. I bring these petitions before You through the mighty name of our Lord Jesus Christ. Amen.

Adapting Psalms into Warfare Prayers

C. Fred Dickason, a former professor at Moody Bible Institute and author of *Winning the War Through Prayer*, suggests patterning some of our warfare prayers after the psalms.[4] Here are some examples:

> With God we shall do valiantly;
>   it is he who will tread down our foes
>   (Psalm 60:12).

> Arise, O LORD, in your anger;
>   lift yourself up against the fury of my enemies;
>   awake for me; you have appointed a judgment...
> Oh, let the evil of the wicked come to an end,
>   and may you establish the righteous...
> My shield is with God,
>   who saves the upright in heart
>   (Psalm 7:6,9,10).

> Arise, O LORD! Confront him, subdue him!
>   Deliver my soul from the wicked by your sword
>   (Psalm 17:13).

But I trust in you, O LORD;
　I say, "You are my God."
My times are in your hand;
　rescue me from the hand of my enemies and from my
　　persecutors!
Make your face shine on your servant;
　save me in your steadfast love!
　　　　　　(Psalm 31:14-16).

Through you we push down our foes;
　through your name we tread down those who rise up
　　against us.
For not in my bow do I trust,
　nor can my sword save me.
But you have saved us from our foes
　and have put to shame those who hate us.
In God we have boasted continually,
　and we will give thanks to your name forever
　　　　　　(Psalm 44:5-8).

As you read through the book of Psalms, always be ready to adapt some psalms into warfare prayers. This can become an important part of your overall strategy in victory during spiritual warfare.

Exhortations to Prayer

I close this chapter with some exhortations on prayer from great saints of the present and the past:[5]

"All our perils are nothing, so long as we have prayer."
　　　　　—Charles Spurgeon

"A prayerless Christian is a powerless Christian."
　　　　　—Billy Graham

"Fight all your battles on your knees and you win every time."
—Charles Stanley

"Prayer is the most important thing in my life. If I should neglect prayer for a single day, I should lose a great deal of the fire of faith."
—Martin Luther

"Trouble and perplexity drive us to prayer, and prayer driveth away trouble and perplexity."
—Philipp Melanchthon

"Pray often; for prayer is a shield to the soul, a sacrifice to God, and a scourge for Satan."
—John Bunyan

13

The Role of Angels

A ngels are "ministering spirits sent out to serve for the sake of those who are to inherit salvation" (Hebrews 1:14). The root meaning of *ministering* has to do with rendering service. God created the angels to render service in various capacities to those who are to inherit salvation. (*That's you and me!*) Since angels are spirits, most of their activities are invisible to us—except when they occasionally take on a human appearance (Hebrews 13:2).

A Survey of Angels in the End Times

God's holy angels will be extremely active in the end times. During the first half of the tribulation period, seven powerful angels will be in charge of the seven trumpet judgments that will bring seven calamities upon the earth, which is Satan's and the antichrist's kingdom (Revelation 8:1,6). With each blowing of a trumpet by an angel, a new judgment falls upon the earth. These judgments will include hail and fire mixed with blood, the sea turning to blood, water turning bitter, various cosmic disturbances, affliction by demonic scorpions, and the death of a third of humankind (Revelation 8:6–9:21). This work of inflicting judgments upon humankind, at God's command, flies in the face of Hollywood's typical portrayal of angels as always being gentle, kind, and benevolent to *all* human beings.

At the midpoint of the tribulation period, a great angelic battle erupts in heaven:

> Now war arose in heaven, Michael and his angels fighting against the dragon. And the dragon and his angels fought back, but he was defeated, and there was no longer any place for them in heaven. And the great dragon was thrown down, that ancient serpent, who is called the devil and Satan, the deceiver of the whole world— he was thrown down to the earth, and his angels were thrown down with him (Revelation 12:7-9).

The holy angels have been contending with fallen angels for a long time. In Daniel 10:13, for example, we read that a demon contended with one of God's holy angels attempting to bring an answer to the prophet Daniel's prayer. Jude 9 informs us that the archangel Michael contended with the devil as they disputed over Moses' body. Contending is nothing new in the world of angels.

The archangel Michael—God's top-ranking angel—will lead the holy angels to victory over Satan and his fallen angels in the heavenly battle described in Revelation 12. The term *archangel* occurs just twice in the New Testament, and in both instances it is singular (1 Thessalonians 4:16; Jude 9). The only archangel identified in the Bible is Michael.

Michael's battle with Satan marks the beginning of the "time of trouble, such as never has been since there was a nation till that

time" (Daniel 12:1). This horrific period—the last half of the tribulation—is the "great tribulation" of which Jesus spoke (Matthew
24:21). At this time Satan will launch a massive campaign of destruction against all Jews. He knows his time is short (Revelation 12:12)—
just three and a half years until Jesus' glorious second coming. He
therefore goes forth with a vengeance in seeking to do as much damage as he can on earth.

Not long after this, another seven angels will be in charge of the
seven bowl judgments that will bring seven final calamities upon
the world, which is Satan's and the antichrist's kingdom (Revelation
16:1). With each new pouring of a bowl by an angel, a new judgment
of God falls upon the world. These judgments will include horri-
bly painful sores on human beings, more bodies of water turning to
blood, the death of all sea creatures, people being scorched by the
sun, rivers drying up, total darkness engulfing the land, a devastat-
ing earthquake, widespread destruction, and much more (Revelation 16).

The holy angels will also accompany Christ at the second coming: "For the Son of Man is going to come with his angels in the
glory of his Father" (Matthew 16:27). "When the Son of Man comes
in his glory, and all the angels with him, then he will sit on his glorious throne" (Matthew 25:31; see also Revelation 19:11-14). At this
time, the Satan-driven antichrist and his forces will be overthrown.

Following the second coming, God's holy angels will gather
believers as a prelude to their entrance into Christ's one-thousand-
year millennial kingdom. Mark 13:26-27 affirms: "They will see the
Son of Man coming in clouds with great power and glory. And then
he will send out the angels and gather his elect from the four winds,
from the ends of the earth to the ends of heaven."

The angels will also gather unbelievers for judgment: "The Son of Man will send his angels, and they will gather out of his kingdom all causes of sin and all law-breakers, and throw them into the fiery furnace" (Matthew 13:40-42; see also 13:49-50).

At this time, a powerful angel will bind Satan with a great chain in the abyss for the duration of Christ's millennial kingdom: "Then I saw an angel coming down from heaven, holding in his hand the key to the bottomless pit and a great chain. And he seized the dragon, that ancient serpent, who is the devil and Satan, and bound him for a thousand years, and threw him into the pit, and shut it and sealed it over him, so that he might not deceive the nations any longer, until the thousand years were ended" (Revelation 20:1-3). After the millennial kingdom, Satan will suffer eternal judgment in the lake of fire (20:10).

Following the millennial kingdom is the eternal state. An angel gave John a personal tour of what awaits believers in the eternal state—including the New Jerusalem (the eternal city of the redeemed), the river of life, and the tree of life (Revelation 21–22). What an awesome sight it must have been for John!

The angel who showed these things to John was so resplendently glorious that John's inclination was to bow down and worship him; but the angel refused. As recounted by John:

> I fell down to worship at the feet of the angel who showed them to me, but he said to me, "You must not do that! I am a fellow servant with you and your brothers the prophets, and with those who keep the words of this book. Worship God" (Revelation 22:8-9).

The angel then gave final instructions to John, and the book of Revelation ends with a promise of Jesus' soon glorious appearing (Revelation 22:12-13,20).

The Multifaceted Ministry of Angels

We know that angels are "ministering spirits" who serve "those who will inherit salvation" (Hebrews 1:14). But in what ways do angels serve the heirs of salvation, both in the present age and in the prophetic future?

The ministry of angels is multifaceted. Among many other things, God may use angels to bring messages to believers (Luke 1:13), answer their prayers (Acts 12:7), guard them from dangers (2 Kings 6:15-17), encourage them in times of danger (Acts 27:23-24), and take care of them at the moment of death (Luke 16:22; Jude 9). John Wesley, the eighteenth-century founder of Methodism, wrote that angels serve believers "in a thousand ways...They may assist us in our searching after truth, remove many doubts and difficulties...They may warn us of evil in disguise, and place what is good in a clear strong light."[1]

Because angels are so active in the believer's life, the late evangelist Billy Graham urges: "Every true believer in Christ should be encouraged and strengthened! Angels are watching; they mark your path. They superintend all the events of your life and protect the interest of the Lord God, always working to promote His plans and to bring about His highest will for you." Graham says that if we "would only realize how close His ministering angels are, what calm assurance we could have in facing the cataclysms of life. While we do not place our faith directly in angels, we should place it in the God who rules the angels; then we can have peace."[2]

In what follows, I address three primary ministries of angels in the present age and into the end times: the ministry of divine messages, the ministry of protection, and the ministry of answering prayer.

The Ministry of Divine Messages

A primary role of the holy angels is as God's messengers, bringing revelation, announcements, warnings, and other information to the people of God. Angels appeared to Lot to warn him about the impending judgment on Sodom (Genesis 19). An angel appeared to the prophet Daniel to reveal the future (Daniel 9). An angel appeared to Zechariah to announce the coming birth of John the Baptist (Luke 1:13). An angel appeared to Joseph and Mary to announce the birth of the Savior, Jesus Christ (Luke 1). An angel appeared to Cornelius and instructed him to send for Simon Peter so Peter could tell him all about salvation in Jesus Christ (Acts 10:3-33). All throughout Scripture, we find angels appearing to humans as God's messengers.[3]

When angels act as messengers, they are always *God's* messengers. They do not act on their own. They serve at the pleasure of the Almighty. The angels "are couriers for Someone other than themselves. They're Someone else's ambassadors, Someone else's agents. They represent only Him, and never themselves. They are channels to carry only His information. They speak and act according to His instructions and they bear His authority."[4]

Angels continue their role as God's messengers in the end times. In Revelation 14:6-7, for example, we read: "Then I saw another angel flying directly overhead, with an eternal gospel to proclaim to those who dwell on earth, to every nation and tribe and language and people. And he said with a loud voice, 'Fear God and give him glory, because the hour of his judgment has come, and worship him who made heaven and earth, the sea and the springs of water.'"

Revelation 14:9-11 then tells us that "another angel" said with a loud voice:

If anyone worships the beast and its image and receives a mark on his forehead or on his hand, he also will drink the wine of God's wrath, poured full strength into the cup of his anger, and he will be tormented with fire and sulfur in the presence of the holy angels and in the presence of the Lamb. And the smoke of their torment goes up forever and ever, and they have no rest, day or night, these worshipers of the beast and its image, and whoever receives the mark of its name.

This angel called for the "endurance of the saints" (verse 12).

Toward the end of the tribulation period, an angel from heaven will deliver a message about the judgment of New Babylon and its fall: "Fallen, fallen is Babylon the great" (Revelation 18:2; compare with 14:8). This judgment will be catastrophic.

The Ministry of Protection

Angels have acted as guardians for Christians through the ages. Scholars disagree, however, about whether every Christian has his or her own guardian angel, or whether angels as a company guard over Christians in a more general sense.

Two primary passages in the New Testament relate to guardian angels. Matthew 18:10 says, "See that you do not despise one of these little ones. For I tell you that in heaven their angels always see the face of my Father who is in heaven." In Acts 12:15, we find a woman named Rhoda recognizing Peter's voice outside the door of a house. The others inside the house—thinking Peter was still in jail—replied: "You are out of your mind...It is his angel." Some Christian scholars conclude from these two verses that every believer must have his or her own guardian angel.

Many of the early church fathers believed every individual is under the care of a particular angel assigned to him or her as a guardian. The great philosopher and theologian Thomas Aquinas likewise affirmed that each person has a guardian angel assigned to him or her at birth. Prior to birth, Aquinas said, the child in the womb falls under the care of the mother's guardian angel.[5]

It is possible that each believer has a specific guardian angel assigned to him or her. Other theologians dispute this, claiming that Matthew 18:10 and Acts 12:15 are flimsy support for this idea. They note that the angels of the little ones in Matthew 18:10 are in heaven, not with the little ones. It is more likely, they say, that multitudes of angels are always ready and willing to render help and protection to each individual Christian as the need arises.

Consider 2 Kings 6, where we find Elisha and his servant on a mountain surrounded by enemy troops. The servant said, "Alas, my master! What shall we do?" (verse 15). Elisha replied, "'Do not be afraid, for those who are with us are more than those who are with them.' Then Elisha prayed and said, 'O LORD, please open his eyes that he may see'" (verses 16-17). The servant then beheld countless glorious angels surrounding him and his master so that the enemies could not get through to them.

We also recall that Jesus could have called on twelve legions of angels to rescue Him if He had wanted (Matthew 26:53). A single Roman legion had six thousand soldiers. This means Jesus could have easily summoned seventy-two thousand angels to come to His aid if He so desired.

Psalm 91:9-11 records this promise from God:

> Because you have made the LORD your dwelling place—
> the Most High, who is my refuge—

No evil shall be allowed to befall you,
    no plague come near your tent.
For he will command his angels concerning you
    to guard you in all your ways.

This passage supports the idea that countless angels of God are always ready and willing to help Christians if the need arises.

The great Reformer and theologian John Calvin offers us this balanced perspective:

> Whether individual angels have been assigned to individual believers for their protection, I dare not affirm with confidence...Specific angels have been appointed as guardians over kingdoms and provinces. Christ also, when he says that the children's angels always behold the Father's face (Matthew 18:10), hints that there are certain angels to whom their safety has been committed. But from this I do not know whether one ought to infer that each individual has the protection of his own angel. We ought to hold as a fact that the care of each one of us is not the task of one angel only, but all with one consent watch over our salvation.[6]

Calvin suggests we should feel happy and confident knowing that many angels are constantly guarding us, rather than feel discouraged because we do not each have an individual angel: "If the fact that all the heavenly host are keeping watch for his safety will not satisfy a man, I do not see what benefit he could derive from knowing that one angel has been given to him as his special guardian."[7]

I think James Montgomery Boice is spot on in affirming that if we as Christians were more fully aware of God's provision of angelic protection—regardless of whether it involves one or many angels—we would be less fearful of our circumstances and enemies.[8] This includes enemies such as the rulers, the authorities, the cosmic powers over this present darkness, and the spiritual forces of evil in the heavenly places (Ephesians 6:12).

Our big problem is our tendency to walk by sight and not by faith. The walk of faith recognizes God's constant provision of angelic protection.

Angels continue their role as protectors of God's people in the end times. For example, in Revelation 18:2-3, John hears an angel announcing judgment upon New Babylon. Then John hears "another voice from heaven"—apparently another angel—warning God's people in New Babylon: "Come out of her, my people, lest you take part in her sins, lest you share in her plagues" (18:4). The angel, acting in the capacity of a guardian, urges God's people to exit New Babylon quickly so they can escape the judgments that are about to fall upon the wicked city.

This reminds us of how angels appeared to Lot and urged him to get out of Sodom before God's judgment fell upon the city: "As morning dawned, the angels urged Lot, saying, 'Up! Take your wife and your two daughters who are here, lest you be swept away in the punishment of the city'" (Genesis 19:15). In both ancient times and in the prophetic future, one important role of God's angels is to warn believers to escape judgment.

In keeping with the biblical teaching on guardian angels, Daniel 12:1 reveals that the archangel Michael is the special guardian and protector assigned to Israel, especially during the future tribulation period. This is no doubt one reason a remnant of the Jews will survive the tribulation, despite the best efforts of Satan and the antichrist to destroy them.

The Ministry of Answering Prayer

God does not have to depend on angels to answer the prayers of His people. He often answers prayers apart from any angelic involvement (1 Chronicles 5:20; 1 Peter 3:12). Other times He uses angels to answer prayers.

We find an example in Acts 12. Peter was in prison. While there, "earnest prayer for him was made to God by the church" (verse 5). An angel shortly after appeared in Peter's prison cell and helped him escape:

> An angel…struck Peter on the side and woke him, saying, "Get up quickly." And the chains fell off his hands. And the angel said to him, "Dress yourself and put on your sandals." And he did so. And he said to him, "Wrap your cloak around you and follow me." And he went out and followed him. He did not know that what was being done by the angel was real, but thought he was seeing a vision. When they had passed the first and the second guard, they came to the iron gate leading into the city. It opened for them of its own accord, and they went out and went along one street, and immediately the angel left him (Acts 12:7-10).

This is a clear example of Christians praying to God and God immediately responding by dispatching an angel to grant the request. We assume God sometimes answers our prayers in this way as well.

We also do well to remember that demons (fallen angels) sometimes seek to thwart the angels God uses in answering prayers. As I've mentioned previously, a fallen angel detained a holy angel God assigned to answer Daniel's prayer (Daniel 10:13). Only when the archangel Michael came to the rescue was the lesser holy angel freed to carry out his task.

God continues to use angels in the end times to bring answers to prayer among God's people. One good example is in Revelation 6:9, where we read of Christian martyrs whose souls are in heaven: "I saw under the altar the souls of those who had been slain for the word of God and for the witness they had borne." These martyrs prayed to God: "O Sovereign Lord, holy and true, how long before you will judge and avenge our blood on those who dwell on the earth?" (6:10). Angels play a major role in bringing about the answer to this prayer. Seven angels will inflict the seven trumpet judgments upon the earth (8:1,6), and seven other angels will inflict the seven bowl judgments upon the earth (16:1). The martyrs pray to God for judgment. The angels—under God's providential direction—inflict judgment.

An Exhortation

My friends, one day we as Christians will dwell with Christ face-to-face in His unveiled, glorious presence. When we receive our glorified resurrection bodies, the perishable will have become imperishable and the mortal will have become immortal (1 Corinthians 15:50-53). In our present bodies, we cannot endure the direct presence of the triune God—His glory is too great, too overwhelming. But our resurrection bodies (our body upgrades) will be specially suited to dwell in His presence.

Scripture tells us that even now, Christ is preparing an eternal, glorious dwelling place for us (John 14:1-3). If the present created universe with its incredible starry host is any indication of what Christ can do (John 1:3; Colossians 1:16; Hebrews 1:2,10), then this eternal dwelling place must be astounding (see 1 Corinthians 2:9).

When we enter glory, we will perceive angels just as clearly as you and I perceive each other here on earth (1 Corinthians 13:12). We will see them just as they see us. And we will jointly serve our glorious King—Jesus Christ—from eternity to eternity, from age to age forevermore.

Let this future reality be an encouragement to you in the present. As you face the powers of darkness in spiritual warfare, never forget that God's secret agents—the angels—are working behind the scenes on your behalf. God's angels are for you, the Father is for you, the Son is for you, and the Holy Spirit is for you.

You are not alone in the battle.

Postscript

We've covered a tremendous amount of important ground in this book. I pray it has been both educational and a blessing to you. As we bring our little journey to a close, I think it would be beneficial to bring together the highlights of what we've learned. These are the things I really want you to remember.

You Have Enemies!

- You and I have enemies—ferocious, invisible enemies. Paul describes them as the rulers, the authorities, the cosmic powers over this present darkness, and the spiritual forces of evil in the heavenly places (Ephesians 6:12). These are various ranks of evil spirits, and they all follow Satan's lead.

- The names and titles used of Satan reveal his character. He is the accuser of believers, an adversary likened to a roaring lion, a murderer, the devil (meaning "slanderer"), the god of this world, the tempter, Beelzebul (the "lord of filth"), the father of lies, the enemy, the evil one, and the serpent. He is a formidable nemesis.

- Satan and his host of fallen angels (demons) have developed specific tactics (schemes) to bring Christians down—or, if I may be more direct, to bring *you* down. Satan has a game plan to ruin your life.

- Satan has been observing human beings on earth ever since Adam and Eve were first created. That means he has vast experience about the most effective ways to bring Christians down.

- Satan is on a leash. He cannot go beyond what our sovereign God will permit.

- We should respect our enemy but not fear him. If we rightly fear (or reverence) God, we need not fear anyone else.

- Satan and demons are very active in the present age, but their activity will increase notably in the end times.

You Are in a War

- Spiritual warfare is raging all around us (2 Corinthians 10:3-5).

- Spiritual warfare is an integral part of the Christian experience. It is a fact of life. To think a Christian could avoid spiritual warfare is like imagining that a gardener could avoid dealing with weeds.

- In spiritual warfare, Christians should "wage the good warfare" (1 Timothy 1:18), "fight the good fight of the faith" (1 Timothy 6:12), and be a "good soldier of Christ Jesus" (2 Timothy 2:3).

- In this war, you are a targeted person. There's a bull's-eye on your back. You are being stalked. Satan is locked and loaded, and his bullets have your name on them.

- Not every Christian is at equal risk as a target of Satan. Christians who seek to live for Christ—those who obey Him and shine His light in a dark world—are at highest risk from the powers of darkness.

- As a Christian soldier, you must be spiritually prepared for battle.

Our Enemies Have Allies

- Scripture reveals that Satan has two powerful allies in accomplishing his dastardly deeds among human beings:

  One ally is *the world*—an anti-God, anti-Christian system headed by Satan. It offers many allurements to distract Christians away from God.

  A second ally is *the flesh*—the sinful force within each of us that is in total rebellion against God.

- Just as allies play a critical role in any war, so the world and the flesh play a critical role in the devil's goal of overcoming and defeating Christians.

Our Enemies Use Tactics Against Us

- Satan's primary tactic is to target our minds. He knows that our thoughts determine our actions.

- Satan is relentless. He never gives up. If one tactic does not work against us, he will try another.

- A common tactic of Satan is to keep us from focusing on our standing "in Christ" and to tempt us instead to focus on the imagined requirement to do many good works to keep pleasing God. Such efforts are futile. We always fail when we try to earn God's favor by good works. When we fail, Satan accuses our consciences and makes us feel like worms before God.

- Satan vigorously flings a variety of "flaming darts" at us (Ephesians 6:16).

- Satan may attempt to neutralize our Christian lives by a flaming dart of discouragement or depression or doubts about God, the Bible, or salvation.

- Satan may also attempt to neutralize our lives as Christians by a flaming dart of worry, including worry about failures of the past, potential failures of the future, and death, which could come at any time. He wants us to worry in the present as we agonize over the past and the future.

- Satan may tempt us to succumb to unrighteous anger, for this will open the door for deeper demonic affliction.

- Satan may tempt us to take personal offense at others.

- Satan will relentlessly seek to rob us of our joy in the Lord.

- Satan may attempt to neutralize our lives as Christians by tempting us to have self-generated pride.

- Satan seeks to incite us to take a minimalist view toward sin.

- Satan seeks to incite us to commit sexual sins out of a lack of self-control.

- Satan seeks to inflict sickness and disease upon our bodies.

- Satan seeks to incite persecution—even martyrdom—against Christians in different parts of the world.

- Satan seeks to destroy Christian churches and ministries via his highly effective tactic of *divide and conquer*.

- Satan seeks to motivate and generate apostasy in the church.

- Satan is a master niche marketer of false ideas. There's something for everyone in the kingdom of the cults. Satan provides a variety of deceptive options to satisfy people's varied desires. The goal in marketing these cultic ideas is to keep people away from the true God, the true Jesus, and the true gospel.

- As bad as spiritual warfare is in the present age, it will grow increasingly worse as we move into the end times. It will reach its greatest climax during the seven-year tribulation period.

God's Provisions for Our Victory

The most important component in our victory over the powers of darkness is *our position in Christ.* The best way to keep the enemy *out* is to keep Christ *in*. We are not fighting *for* victory but *from* victory, for *Jesus has already defeated Satan*! Living our Christian lives "in Christ" is our number one defense. Never forget this. Imprint this truth upon your mind!

The *Holy Spirit*—our divine "Helper" (John 14:16)—is always at our side during our struggles in spiritual warfare. His power enables us not only to stand against Satan and his tactics but also to live righteously so that Satan finds it harder to penetrate our lives. His role as the "Spirit of truth" helps us combat Satan's lies and deceptions. We must never forget: "He who is in you [the Holy Spirit] is greater than he who is in the world [Satan]" (1 John 4:4).

God has provided *spiritual armor* for our defense in spiritual warfare (Ephesians 6:10-18). Each piece of armor is important and serves a special purpose. But you and I must put on this armor. God does not force us to dress in it. Wearing this armor means that righteousness, obedience to the will of God, faith in God, and an effective use of the Word of God will characterize our lives. We must put on this armor every day.

The effective use of *the Word of God* is especially important. The Word of God is the "Word of truth" (2 Timothy 2:15), inspired by the Holy Spirit (the "Spirit of truth"—John 16:13), and centers on Jesus Christ ("the way, and the truth, and the life"—John 14:6). It is important to *know* God's Word, to *meditate* on God's Word, to *memorize* God's Word, and to *obey* God's Word (see Psalm 119).

God's Word emphasizes the need for us to pray daily for ourselves and for our fellow Christian brothers and sisters. *Prayer* is our primary means of bringing our needs—including those relating to our battles in spiritual warfare—before the throne of grace and power. We can model many of our warfare prayers on the psalms in the Old Testament. We can also put on God's spiritual armor through prayer.

God has assigned His *angels* to engage in various ministries in our lives, including guarding over us, providing comfort when we feel endangered, and answering our prayers (under God's direction).

There is no telling how many times God's invisible "secret agents" have helped us throughout our Christian lives.

Closing Tidbits of Advice from Christian Leaders

I can think of no better way to close this book than to provide some final words of advice from respected Christian leaders:

Kay Arthur: "The first rule of battle is this: know your enemy. A thorough knowledge of the opponent's strength, his probable line of attack, and his tactics are vital to achieving victory."[1]

David Jeremiah: "Satan's main goal is to destroy the faith of Christians by getting us to doubt God's goodness, love, forgiveness, protection, provision, and promises. When Satan choreographs difficult circumstances in our lives, it is not just to inflict pain; it is for the purpose of destroying our trust in God."[2]

Mark Hitchcock: "When we fear God, we don't fear other things. The person who fears God has no need to fear anything else. When Christ is great, our fears are not. As fear of God expands, fears about life and death diminish, including the fear of Satan."[3]

Warren Wiersbe: "It is good to reaffirm our surrender to God at the beginning of each day. When you first awaken, immediately give your body to God as an act of faith...The next step is to reach for your Bible and present your mind to God for spiritual renewal. It is the Word of God that renews the mind and transforms it...After you have given God your body (and gotten out of bed) and your mind (and meditated on the Word), your next step is to give him your will; and this you do in prayer."[4]

C. Fred Dickason: "Victory demands submission to our Captain and obedience to His commands. We cannot love the world and God at the same time (James 4:4; 1 John 2:15). We cannot have victory over the greatest of all rebels if we ourselves are rebels."[5]

Randy Alcorn: "Life on earth is a dot, a brief window of opportunity; life in Heaven (and ultimately on the New Earth) is a line going out from that dot for eternity. If we're smart, we'll live not for the dot, but for the line."[6] An eternal perspective strengthens us amid our battles in spiritual warfare.

Heavenly Father, thank You for alerting me about the spiritual enemies who stand against me. And thank You for informing me about the various tactics the powers of darkness utilize to injure me spiritually, emotionally, and physically.

Please give me discernment so I can understand what I need to know about the world, the flesh, and the devil. And please give me the resources I need to stand strong against this gang attack.

I pray that You neutralize the flaming darts of the evil one in my life. Protect my mind by the truth of Your Word. Help me understand increasingly more about my position "in Christ," and how this is a key to my spiritual victory. Enable me to keep my spiritual armor on at all times. Enable me to walk in perpetual dependence on the Holy Spirit. And please bless my prayer life.

I ask all this in Jesus' name.

Amen.

Key Bible Verses on Our Position in Christ

John 1:12—Believing in Jesus makes us children of God.

John 15:5—Abiding in Jesus produces fruit in our lives.

John 15:15—We are friends of Jesus.

Romans 5:1—We have peace with God through Jesus.

Romans 6:6—Our sinful self was crucified with Christ.

Romans 8:1—There is no condemnation for those in Christ.

Romans 8:14-15—We are adopted into God's family.

Romans 8:16—We are children of God.

Romans 8:31—If God is for us, who can be against us?

Romans 8:37—We are more than conquerors through Christ.

Romans 8:38-39—Nothing can separate us from God's love in Christ.

Romans 13:14—We can "wear" Jesus like a suit and overcome the flesh.

1 Corinthians 3:16—Christians are God's temple.

1 Corinthians 6:17—We are in union with Jesus.

1 Corinthians 6:19-20—Our bodies are a temple of the Holy Spirit.

2 Corinthians 1:21-22—We are sealed by the Holy Spirit.

2 Corinthians 2:14—Christ always leads us in triumphal procession.

2 Corinthians 5:17—We are new creatures in Christ.

2 Corinthians 12:9—Christ's grace is sufficient for us in our weakness.

Galatians 2:20—Christ lives in me.

Galatians 3:26-28—We are in God's family.

Ephesians 1:3—We have been blessed with every spiritual blessing in the heavenlies.

Ephesians 1:5—We are in God's family.

Ephesians 1:7—We are redeemed and forgiven in Christ.

Ephesians 1:11—We have a heavenly inheritance waiting for us.

Ephesians 2:4-5—We have been made alive together with Christ.

Ephesians 2:6—We are seated with Christ in the heavenly places.

Ephesians 2:13—In Christ we are "brought near."

Ephesians 2:19—We are members of God's household.

Ephesians 4:24—Our new self is in God's likeness.

Philippians 4:13—We can do all things through Christ.

Philippians 4:19—God will supply all our needs in Christ.

Colossians 3:1-3—We have been raised with Christ.

2 Timothy 1:7—God gave us a spirit not of fear but of power and love and self-control.

Hebrews 4:15-16—We can boldly approach the throne of grace.

1 Peter 1:23—We are born again.

Bibliography

1. Christian Books on Angels and Demons

Anderson, Neil. *Victory Over the Darkness: Realize the Power of Your Identity in Christ*. Minneapolis: Bethany House, 2000.

Anderson, Neil, and Timothy Warner. *The Essential Guide to Spiritual Warfare*. Minneapolis: Bethany House, 2000.

Arnold, Clinton E. *Three Crucial Questions About Spiritual Warfare*. Grand Rapids, MI: Baker, 1997.

———. *Powers of Darkness: Principalities and Powers in Paul's Letters*. Downers Grove, IL: InterVarsity, 1992.

Arthur, Kay. *Spiritual Warfare: Overcoming the Enemy*. Colorado Springs: Waterbrook, 2011.

Barnhouse, Donald. *The Invisible War*. Grand Rapids: Zondervan, 1980.

Bevere, John. *The Bait of Satan: Living Free from the Deadly Trap of Offense*. Lake Mary, FL: Charisma House, 2014.

Bubeck, Mark. *Overcoming the Adversary: Warfare Praying Against Demon Activity*. Chicago: Moody, 1984.

———. *Spiritual Warfare Prayers*. Chicago: Moody, 1997.

Chafer, Lewis Sperry. *Satan: His Motive and Methods*. Grand Rapids, MI: Zondervan, 1977.

Dickason, C. Fred. *Angels: Elect and Evil*. Chicago: Moody, 1978.

Evans, Tony. *Prayers for Victory in Spiritual Warfare*. Eugene, OR: Harvest House, 2015.

———. *The Truth about Angels and Demons*. Chicago: Moody, 2005.

————. *Victory in Spiritual Warfare: Outfitting Yourself for the Battle*. Eugene, OR: Harvest House, 2011.

Gaebelein, A.C. *What the Bible Says About Angels*. Grand Rapids, MI: Baker, 1993.

Garrett, Duane. *Angels and the New Spirituality*. Nashville: Broadman and Holman, 1995.

Geisler, Norman L., and Douglas E. Potter. *The Doctrine of Angels and Demons*. Charlotte, NC: Bastion, 2016.

Graham, Billy. *Angels: God's Secret Agents*. New York: Doubleday, 1975.

Gurnall, William. *The Christian in Complete Armour*. Amazon Digital Services, 2010.

Hitchcock, Mark. *101 Answers to Questions About Satan, Demons, and Spiritual Warfare*. Eugene, OR: Harvest House, 2014.

Ice, Thomas, and Robert Dean. *Overrun by Demons*. Eugene, OR: Harvest House, 1990.

Ingram, Chip. *The Invisible War: What Every Believer Needs to Know About Satan, Demons, and Spiritual Warfare*. Grand Rapids, MI: Baker, 2015.

Jeremiah, David. *The Spiritual Warfare Answer Book*. Nashville: Thomas Nelson, 2016.

————. *What the Bible Says About Angels*. Sisters, OR: Multnomah, 1996.

Knowles, Victor. *Angels and Demons*. Joplin, MO: College Press, 1994.

Kreeft, Peter. *Angels (and Demons)*. San Francisco: Ignatius, 2004.

Lewis, C.S. *The Screwtape Letters*. San Francisco: HarperOne, 2009.

Lightner, Robert P. *Angels, Satan and Demons*. Nashville: Thomas Nelson, 1998.

Lindsey, Hal, and Carole C. Carlson. *Satan Is Alive and Well on Planet Earth*. Grand Rapids, MI: Zondervan, 1972.

Lloyd-Jones, D. Martyn. *Spiritual Depression: Its Causes and Cures*. Grand Rapids, MI: Zondervan, 2016.

Lockyer, Herbert. *All the Angels in the Bible*. Peabody, MA: Hendrickson, 1995.

Logan, Jim. *Reclaiming Surrendered Ground: Protecting Your Family from Spiritual Attacks*. Chicago: Moody, 1995.

MacArthur, John F. *The Glory of Heaven: The Truth About Heaven, Angels, and Eternal Life*. Wheaton, IL: Crossway, 1996.

MacDonald, Hope. *When Angels Appear*. Grand Rapids, MI: Zondervan, 1982.

Myers, Edward. *A Study of Angels*. West Monroe, LA: Howard, 1994.

Murphy, Ed. *Handbook for Spiritual Warfare*. Nashville: Thomas Nelson, 1996.

Northrup, L.W. *Encounters with Angels*. Wheaton, IL: Tyndale House, 1993.

Payne, Karl. *Spiritual Warfare*. New York: WND, 2016.

Penn-Lewis, Jessie. *War on the Saints: A History of Satanic Deceptions in Christianity and the Conflict Between Good and Evil*. CreateSpace, 2017.

Pentecost, J. Dwight. *Your Adversary the Devil*. Grand Rapids, MI: Zondervan, 1979.

Richards, Larry. *The Full Armor of God*. Grand Rapids, MI: Chosen, 2013.

Ryrie, Charles. *Balancing the Christian Life*. Chicago: Moody, 1994.

Stedman, Ray C. *Spiritual Warfare*. Waco, TX: Word, 1976.

Stedman, Rick. *Praying the Armor of God*. Eugene, OR: Harvest House, 2015.

Unger, Merrill F. *Biblical Demonology: A Study of Spiritual Forces at Work Today*. Grand Rapids, MI: Kregel, 1994.

———. *Demons in the World Today*. Wheaton, IL: Tyndale House, 1972.

———. *What Demons Can Do to Saints*. Chicago: Moody, 1991.

Wiersbe, Warren. *The Strategy of Satan*. Wheaton, IL: Tyndale House, 2011.

Wiersbe, Warren, compiler. *Classic Sermons on Angels*. Grand Rapids, MI: Kregel, 1998.

2. Theology Books that Include Angelology

Bancroft, Emery H. *Christian Theology*. Grand Rapids, MI: Zondervan, 1976.

Berkhof, Louis. *Manual of Christian Doctrine*. Grand Rapids, MI: Eerdmans, 1983.

———. *Systematic Theology*. Grand Rapids, MI: Eerdmans, 1982.

Boice, James Montgomery. *Foundations of the Christian Faith*. Downers Grove, IL: InterVarsity, 1981.

Buswell, James Oliver. *A Systematic Theology of the Christian Religion*. Grand Rapids, MI: Zondervan, 1979.

Calvin, John. *Institutes of the Christian Religion*. Ed. John T. McNeill. Trans. Ford Lewis Battles. Philadelphia: Westminster, 1960.

Chafer, Lewis Sperry. *Systematic Theology*, 2 vols. Wheaton, IL: Victor, 1988.

————, and John F. Walvoord. *Major Bible Themes*. Grand Rapids, MI: Zondervan, 1975.

Enns, Paul. *The Moody Handbook of Theology*. Chicago: Moody, 1989.

Erickson, Millard J. *Christian Theology*. Grand Rapids, MI: Baker, 1987.

Evans, William, and S. Maxwell Coder. *The Great Doctrines of the Bible*. Chicago: Moody, 1974.

Henry, Carl F.H., ed. *Basic Christian Doctrines*. Grand Rapids, MI: Baker, 1983.

Hodge, Charles. *Systematic Theology*. Ed. Edward N. Gross. Grand Rapids, MI: Baker, 1988.

Hodges, A.A. *Outlines of Theology*. Grand Rapids, MI: Zondervan, 1972.

Lightner, Robert P. *Evangelical Theology*. Grand Rapids, MI: Baker, 1986.

Ryrie, Charles C. *Basic Theology*. Wheaton, IL: Victor, 1986.

————. *A Survey of Bible Doctrine*. Chicago: Moody, 1980.

Strong, Augustus Hopkins. *Systematic Theology*. Old Tappan, NJ: Revell, 1979.

Thiessen, Henry Clarence. *Lectures in Systematic Theology*. Grand Rapids, MI: Eerdmans, 1981.

3. Helpful Commentaries

Barnes, Albert. *Barnes' Notes on the Old and New Testaments*, 2 vols. Grand Rapids, MI: Baker, 1977.

Bruce, F.F., ed. *The International Bible Commentary*. Grand Rapids, MI: Zondervan, 1979.

Gaebelein, Frank E., ed. *The Expositor's Bible Commentary*. Grand Rapids, MI: Zondervan, 1978.

Henry, Matthew. *Commentary on the Whole Bible*. Grand Rapids, MI: Zondervan, 1974.

Jamieson, Robert, A.R. Fausset, and David A. Brown. *A Commentary—Critical, Experimental, and Practical—on the Old and New Testaments*. Grand Rapids, MI: Eerdmans, 1973.

Keener, Craig S. *The IVP Bible Background Commentary: New Testament.* Downers Grove, IL: InterVarsity, 1993.

Keil, C.F., and Franz Delitzsch. *Biblical Commentary on the Old Testament,* 9 vols. Grand Rapids, MI: Eerdmans, 1954.

Pfeiffer, Charles F., and Everett F. Harrison, eds. *The Wycliffe Bible Commentary.* Chicago: Moody, 1974.

Robertson, A.T. *Word Pictures,* 7 vols. Nashville: Broadman, 1930.

Vincent, Marvin R. *Word Studies in the New Testament,* 4 vols. Grand Rapids, MI: Eerdmans, 1975.

Walvoord, John F., and Roy B. Zuck, eds. *The Bible Knowledge Commentary,* 2 vols. Wheaton, IL: Victor, 1985.

Wuest, Kenneth S. *Wuest's Word Studies,* 4 vols. Grand Rapids, MI: Eerdmans, 1953.

4. Helpful Reference Works

Bromiley, Geoffrey, ed. *International Standard Bible Encyclopedia,* 4 vols. Grand Rapids, MI: Eerdmans, 1988.

Brown, Colin, ed. *The New International Dictionary of New Testament Theology,* 3 vols. Grand Rapids, MI: Zondervan, 1979.

Brown, Francis, S.R. Driver, and Charles A. Briggs. *A Hebrew and English Lexicon of the Old Testament.* Oxford, England: Clarendon, 1980.

Douglas, J.D., ed. *The New Bible Dictionary.* Wheaton, IL: Tyndale House, 1982.

Draper, Edythe, ed. *Draper's Book of Quotations for the Christian World.* Grand Rapids, MI: Baker, 1992.

Elwell, Walter A., ed. *Evangelical Dictionary of Theology.* Grand Rapids, MI: Baker, 1984.

———, ed. *Topical Analysis of the Bible.* Grand Rapids, MI: Baker, 1991.

Kittel, Gerhard, and Gerhard Friedrich, eds. *Theological Dictionary of the New Testament.* Abridged by Geoffrey W. Bromiley. Grand Rapids, MI: Eerdmans, 1990.

Leon-Dufour, Xavier, ed. *Dictionary of Biblical Theology.* New York: Seabury, 1983.

Tenney, Merrill C., ed. *The Zondervan Pictorial Encyclopedia of the Bible,* 5 vols. Grand Rapids, MI: Zondervan, 1978.

Vine, W.E., Merrill F. Unger, and William White, Jr., eds. *Vine's Expository Dictionary of Biblical Words.* Nashville: Thomas Nelson, 1985.

Zodhiates, Spiros. *The Complete Word Study Dictionary.* Chattanooga, TN: AMG, 1992.

Endnotes

Introduction: Spiritual Warfare

1. Mark Hitchcock, *101 Answers to Questions About Satan, Demons, and Spiritual Warfare* (Eugene, OR: Harvest House, 2014), Apple iBook edition.

2. Robert P. Lightner, *Evangelical Theology* (Grand Rapids, MI: Baker, 1986), 57.

1—The Reality of Satan in the World Today

1. Elaine Pagels, *The Origin of Satan* (New York: Vintage, 2011).

2. See David Spangler, *Emergence: The Rebirth of the Sacred* (New York: Dell, 1984).

3. In this book, the term *cult* is not intended as a pejorative, inflammatory, or injurious word. The term is used simply as a means of categorizing certain religious or semi-religious groups in modern Western culture. Theologically, a cult is defined as a religious group that derives from a parent world religion (such as Christianity), but in fact departs from that parent religion by denying (explicitly or implicitly) one or more of the essential doctrines of that religion. It is *only* in this sense that the term *cult* is used in this book.

4. See "Response to Mainstream Christianity," Christadelphian website: www.christa delphia.org.

5. Craig Hawkins, "The Many Faces of Satanism," *Forward*, Fall 1986, 1; see also Bob Passantino and Gretchen Passantino, *Satanism* (Grand Rapids, MI: Zondervan, 1995).

6. See Craig Hawkins, *Witchcraft: Exploring the World of Wicca* (Grand Rapids, MI: Baker, 1996).

7. Harold Willmington, "If I Were the Devil," *Baptist Bulletin*, December 1971, 13.

8. Ibid.

9. C.S. Lewis, *The Screwtape Letters* (San Francisco: HarperOne, 2015), 3.

10. Norman L. Geisler, *The Doctrine of Angels and Demons* (Charlotte: Bastion, 2016), Kindle edition.

11. Ibid.

2—The Character and Goal of Satan and His Fallen Angels

1. Erwin W. Lutzer; cited in *Draper's Book of Quotations for the Christian World*, ed. Edythe Draper (Grand Rapids, MI: Baker, 1992), 543.

2. Lewis Sperry Chafer, *Satan* (CreateSpace, 2017), Kindle edition.

3. Thomas Ice and Robert Dean, *Overrun by Demons* (Eugene, OR: Harvest House, 1993), 46.

4. William MacDonald, *Believer's Bible Commentary* (Nashville: Thomas Nelson, 2008), The Bible Study App, Olive Tree Software.

5. *NKJV Study Bible*, eds. Earl D. Radmacher, Ronald B. Allen, H. Wayne House (Nashville: Thomas Nelson, 2013), The Bible Study App, Olive Tree Software.

6. David Jeremiah, *Agents of the Apocalypse* (Carol Stream, IL: Tyndale House, 2014), iBook edition.

7. Ray C. Stedman, *Spiritual Warfare* (Waco, TX: Word Books, 1976), 22.

8. Henry C. Thiessen, *Lectures in Systematic Theology* (Grand Rapids, MI: Eerdmans, 1988), 142.

9. Charles C. Ryrie, *A Survey of Bible Doctrine* (Chicago: Moody, 1980), 94.

10. Charles C. Ryrie, *Basic Theology* (Wheaton, IL: Victor, 1986), 147.

11. Charles C. Ryrie, *Balancing the Christian Life* (Chicago: Moody, 1978), 124.

3—Understanding Spiritual Warfare

1. Clinton Arnold, *Three Crucial Questions about Spiritual Warfare* (Grand Rapids, MI: Baker, 1997), Kindle edition.

2. Billy Graham, *Angels: God's Secret Agents* (Garden City, NY: Doubleday, 1975), 24.

3. Kay Arthur, *Spiritual Warfare* (Colorado Springs: Waterbrook, 2011), Kindle edition.

4. Mark Hitchcock, *101 Answers to Questions About Satan, Demons, and Spiritual Warfare* (Eugene, OR: Harvest House, 2014), Apple iBook edition.

5. J.C. Ryle, *Holiness* (Chicago: Moody, n.d.), 115.

6. Chip Ingram, *The Invisible War: What Every Believer Needs to Know about Satan, Demons, and Spiritual Warfare* (Grand Rapids, MI: Baker, 2015), Kindle edition.

7. Arnold, *Three Crucial Questions about Spiritual Warfare*.

8. J. Dwight Pentecost, *God's Answers to Man's Problems* (Chicago: Moody, 1985), 9.

9. Larry Richards, *Full Armor of God* (Grand Rapids, MI: Chosen, 2013), Kindle edition.

10. Warren W. Wiersbe, *The Strategy of Satan* (Wheaton, IL: Tyndale House, 2011), Kindle edition.

11. Charles C. Ryrie, *Study-Graph: Bible Doctrine II* (Chicago: Moody, 1965).

12. Charles C. Ryrie, *A Survey of Bible Doctrine* (Chicago: Moody, 1972), Apple iBook edition.

4—Satan's Schemes: Flaming Darts, Mind Games, Guilt, and Discouragement

1. Larry Richards, *Full Armor of God* (Grand Rapids, MI: Chosen, 2013), Kindle edition.

2. David Jeremiah, *The Spiritual Warfare Answer Book* (Nashville: Thomas Nelson, 2016), Kindle edition.

3. Mark Hitchcock, *101 Answers to Questions About Satan, Demons, and Spiritual Warfare* (Eugene, OR: Harvest House, 2014), Apple iBook edition.

4. Billy Graham, "Answers," October 19, 2009, Billy Graham Evangelistic Association, billygraham.org/answer/where-do-evil-thoughts-come-from-does-satan-put-them -there-sometimes-i-think-he-must-because-they-just-seem-to-pop-into-my-head -without-any-effort-on-my-part-in-any-case-how-are-we-supposed-to-de/.

5. Hank Hanegraaff, "Does Satan Have Access to Our Minds?," December 29, 2010. Article posted at Christian Research Institute, www.equip.org/bible_answers/does -satan-have-access-to-our-minds-2/.

6. Kay Arthur, *Spiritual Warfare* (Colorado Springs: Waterbrook, 2012), Kindle edition.

7. Karl Payne, *Spiritual Warfare* (New York: WND, 2016), Apple iBook edition.

8. Richards, *Full Armor of God*; see also Chip Ingram, *The Invisible War: What Every Believer Needs to Know About Satan, Demons, and Spiritual Warfare* (Grand Rapids, MI: Baker, 2015), Kindle edition.

9. Clinton Arnold, *Three Crucial Questions about Spiritual Warfare* (Grand Rapids, MI: Baker, 1997), Kindle edition.

10. C. Fred Dickason, *Angels: Elect and Evil* (Chicago: Moody, 1978), Kindle edition.

5—Satan's Schemes: Depression, Doubts, Worry, Anger, Personal Offense, and Robbing Joy

1. D. Martyn Lloyd-Jones, *Spiritual Depression: Its Causes and Cures* (Grand Rapids, MI: Zondervan, 2016), Kindle edition.

2. Ibid.

3. Chip Ingram, *The Invisible War: What Every Believer Needs to Know About Satan, Demons, and Spiritual Warfare* (Grand Rapids, MI: Baker, 2015), Kindle edition.

4. Robert Lightner, *Angels, Satan, and Demons* (Nashville: Word, 1998), 81.

5. Corrie ten Boom with John and Elizabeth Sherrill, *The Hiding Place* (New York: Bantam, 1984), Kindle edition.

6. Warren W. Wiersbe, *The Strategy of Satan* (Wheaton, IL: Tyndale House, 2011), Kindle edition.

7. John Bevere, *The Bait of Satan: Living Free from the Deadly Trap of Offense* (Lake Mary, FL: Charisma House, 2014), Kindle edition. Please note that Bevere is in the Word Faith camp, and I do not agree with all that he teaches. But I believe he is correct in his assessment of how spiritually dangerous it can be to hold on to personal offense.

8. Bevere, *The Bait of Satan*.

9. George Müller as cited in Ron Rhodes, *1001 Unforgettable Quotes* (Eugene, OR: Harvest House, 2011), Apple iBook edition.

6—Satan's Schemes: Pride, Hindering Prayer, Sin, and Causing Division

1. Warren W. Wiersbe, *The Strategy of Satan* (Wheaton, IL: Tyndale House, 2011), Kindle edition.

2. Jim Logan, *Reclaiming Surrendered Ground* (Chicago: Moody, 1995), Kindle edition.

3. Randy Alcorn, *Seeing the Unseen: A Daily Dose of Eternal Perspective* (Colorado Springs: Multnomah, 2017), Kindle edition.

4. William Gurnall, *The Christian in Complete Armour* (Amazon Digital Services, 2010), Kindle edition.

5. John Owen as cited in Ron Rhodes, *1001 Unforgettable Quotes* (Eugene, OR: Harvest House, 2011), Apple iBook edition.

6. Thomas Watson as cited in Rhodes, *1001 Unforgettable Quotes*.

7. J.I. Packer as cited in Rhodes, *1001 Unforgettable Quotes*.

8. Morgan Lee, "Here's How 770 Pastors Describe Their Struggle with Porn," *Christianity Today*, January 26, 2016, online edition.

9. Ibid.

10. Maria Cowell, "Porn: Women Use It Too," *Christianity Today*, October 19, 2016, online edition.

11. Ibid.

12. Ibid.

13. Ibid.

14. Samuel Smith, "Pastor Saying Premarital Sex Is OK Pushes People Away from God, Greg Laurie Warns," *Christian Post*, August 29, 2016, online edition.

15. These reviews and endorsements are posted at Amazon.com.

16. Merrill F. Unger, *What Demons Can Do to Saints* (Chicago: Moody, 1991), Kindle edition.

17. Tony Evans, *Victory in Spiritual Warfare* (Eugene, OR: Harvest House, 2011), Kindle edition.

18. David Jeremiah, *The Spiritual Warfare Answer Book* (Nashville: Thomas Nelson, 2016), Kindle edition.

7—Satan's Schemes: Hindering Through Other People, Bodily Illness, Attacking Churches, and Apostasy

1. John Phillips, *Exploring Ephesians and Philippians: An Expository Commentary* (Grand Rapids, MI: Kregel, 1995), 187.

2. Warren W. Wiersbe, *The Strategy of Satan* (Wheaton, IL: Tyndale House, 2011), Kindle edition.

3. See www.recoveringfromreligion.org/.

8—Satan's Schemes: False Religions, Persecution, and Reducing Religious Freedom

1. When I use the word *cult* in this book, it is not intended as a pejorative, inflammatory, or injurious word. The term is used simply as a theological means of categorizing certain religious or semireligious groups in modern America. Theologically speaking, a cult is a religious group that emerges out of a parent world religion (such as Christianity), but in fact departs from that parent religion by denying—explicitly or implicitly—one or more of the essential doctrines of that religion. These essential doctrines include God, Jesus, and the gospel that saves.

2. Emanuel Swedenborg, cited in Cyriel Sigstedt, *The Swedenborg Epic* (New York: Bookman, 1952), 198.

3. Robert J. Morgan, "The World's War on Christianity," *Huffington Post*, March 16, 2014, online edition.

4. Ruth Gledhill, "Report on Freedom of Religion Shows Horrific Persecution of Christians Worldwide," *Christianity Today*, July 1, 2016, online edition.

5. David Kinnaman and Gabe Lyons, *Good Faith: Being a Christian When Society Thinks You're Irrelevant and Extreme* (Grand Rapids, MI: Baker, 2016), 51.

6. Raymond Ibrahim, *Crucified Again: Exposing Islam's New War on Christians* (Washington, DC: Regnery, 2013), Kindle edition.

9—Our Position in Christ

1. Mark Hitchcock, *101 Answers to Questions About Satan, Demons, and Spiritual Warfare* (Eugene, OR: Harvest House, 2014), Apple iBook edition.

2. Mark I. Bubeck, *Warfare Praying* (Chicago: Moody, 2016), Apple iBook edition.

3. David Jeremiah, *The Spiritual Warfare Answer Book* (Nashville: Thomas Nelson, 2016), Kindle edition.

4. Ray Stedman, *From Guilt to Glory*, vol. 21 (Waco, TX: Word, 1978), 136.

5. Charles C. Ryrie, *The Ryrie Study Bible* (Chicago: Moody, 2012), in The Bible Study App, Olive Tree Software.

6. Warren W. Wiersbe, *The Strategy of Satan* (Wheaton, IL: Tyndale House, 2011), Kindle edition.

7. Kay Arthur, *Spiritual Warfare* (Colorado Springs: Waterbrook, 2011), Kindle edition.

8. Chip Ingram, *The Invisible War: What Every Believer Needs to Know About Satan, Demons, and Spiritual Warfare* (Grand Rapids, MI: Baker, 2015), Kindle edition.

9. Tony Evans, *Victory in Spiritual Warfare* (Eugene, OR: Harvest House, 2011), Kindle edition.

10. Merrill F. Unger, *What Demons Can Do to Saints* (Chicago: Moody, 1991), Kindle edition.

11. C. Fred Dickason, *Angels: Elect and Evil* (Chicago: Moody, 1978), Kindle edition.

12. A.W. Tozer, *Born After Midnight* (Harrisburg, PA: Christian Publications, 1959), 43.

13. Hitchcock, *101 Answers to Questions About Satan, Demons, and Spiritual Warfare*.

14. Rick Stedman, *Praying the Armor of God* (Eugene, OR: Harvest House, 2015), Apple iBook edition.

10—The Role of the Holy Spirit

1. William Arndt and Wilbur Gingrich, *A Greek-English Lexicon of the New Testament and Other Early Christian Literature* (Chicago: University of Chicago, 1957), 146.

11—The Armor of God

1. David Jeremiah, *The Spiritual Warfare Answer Book* (Nashville: Thomas Nelson, 2016), Kindle edition.

2. Tony Evans, *Prayers for Victory in Spiritual Warfare* (Eugene, OR: Harvest House, 2015), Apple iBook edition.

3. Warren W. Wiersbe, *The Strategy of Satan* (Wheaton, IL: Tyndale House, 2011), Kindle edition.

4. Ray C. Stedman, *Spiritual Warfare* (Waco, TX: Word, 1976), 114.

5. Rick Stedman, *Praying the Armor of God* (Eugene, OR: Harvest House, 2015), Apple iBook edition.

12—The Role of Prayer

1. William McDonald, *Believer's Bible Commentary* (Nashville: Thomas Nelson, 2008), Bible Study App, Olive Tree Software.

2. Ibid.

3. Tony Evans, *Prayers for Victory in Spiritual Warfare* (Eugene, OR: Harvest House, 2015), Apple iBook edition.

4. C. Fred Dickason, *Winning the War Through Prayer* (Bloomington, IN: WestBow, 2016), Apple iBook edition.

5. All quotes are derived from Ron Rhodes, *1001 Unforgettable Quotes About God, Faith, and the Bible* (Eugene, OR: Harvest House, 2011), iBooks edition.

13—The Role of Angels

1. John Wesley cited in David Connolly, *In Search of Angels: A Celestial Sourcebook for Beginning Your Journey* (New York: Perigee, 1993), 48.

2. Billy Graham, *Angels: God's Secret Agents* (Nashville: Thomas Nelson, 2011), 92, 95, 15.

3. William H. Baker, "Our Chariots of Fire," *Moody Monthly*, January 1986, 36.

4. David Jeremiah, *What the Bible Says About Angels* (Sisters, OR: Multnomah, 1996), 58.

5. Cited in Millard J. Erickson, *Christian Theology* (Grand Rapids, MI: Baker, 1987), 435.

6. John Calvin, *Institutes of the Christian Religion*, ed. John T. McNeill, trans. Ford Lewis Battles (Philadelphia: Westminster, 1960), 1.14.7.

7. Ibid.

8. James Montgomery Boice, *Foundations of the Christian Faith* (Downers Grove, IL: InterVarsity, 1981), 170.

Postscript

1. Kay Arthur, *Spiritual Warfare* (Colorado Springs: Waterbrook, 2011), Kindle edition.

2. David Jeremiah, *The Spiritual Warfare Answer Book* (Nashville: Thomas Nelson, 2016), Kindle edition.

3. Mark Hitchcock, *101 Answers to Questions About Satan, Demons, and Spiritual Warfare* (Eugene, OR: Harvest House, 2014), Apple iBook edition.

4. Warren W. Wiersbe, *The Strategy of Satan* (Wheaton, IL: Tyndale House, 2011), Kindle edition.

5. C. Fred Dickason, *Angels: Elect and Evil* (Chicago: Moody, 1978), Kindle edition.

6. Randy Alcorn, *Seeing the Unseen: A Daily Dose of Eternal Perspective* (Colorado Springs: Multnomah, 2017), Kindle edition.

Other Great Harvest House Books by Ron Rhodes

BOOKS ABOUT THE BIBLE

40 Days Through Genesis

The Big Book of Bible Answers

Bite-Size Bible® Answers

Bite-Size Bible® Charts

Bite-Size Bible® Definitions

Bite-Size Bible® Handbook

Commonly Misunderstood Bible Verses

The Complete Guide to Bible Translations

Find It Fast in the Bible

The Popular Dictionary of Bible Prophecy

Understanding the Bible from A to Z

What Does the Bible Say About…?

BOOKS ABOUT THE END TIMES

8 Great Debates of Bible Prophecy

40 Days Through Revelation

Cyber Meltdown

The End Times in Chronological Order

Northern Storm Rising

Unmasking the Antichrist

BOOKS ABOUT OTHER IMPORTANT TOPICS

5-Minute Apologetics for Today

1001 Unforgettable Quotes About God, Faith, and the Bible

Answering the Objections of Atheists, Agnostics, and Skeptics

Christianity According to the Bible

The Complete Guide to Christian Denominations

Conversations with Jehovah's Witnesses

Find It Quick Handbook on Cults and New Religions

The Truth Behind Ghosts, Mediums, and Psychic Phenomena

Secret Life of Angels

What Happens After Life?

Why Do Bad Things Happen If God Is Good?

Wonder of Heaven

THE 10 MOST IMPORTANT THINGS SERIES

The 10 Most Important Things You Can Say to a Catholic
The 10 Most Important Things You Can Say to a Jehovah's Witness
The 10 Most Important Things You Can Say to a Mason
The 10 Most Important Things You Can Say to a Mormon
The 10 Things You Need to Know About Islam
The 10 Things You Should Know About the Creation vs. Evolution Debate

QUICK REFERENCE GUIDES

Halloween: What You Need to Know
Islam: What You Need to Know
Jehovah's Witnesses: What You Need to Know

THE REASONING FROM THE SCRIPTURES SERIES

Reasoning from the Scriptures with Catholics
Reasoning from the Scriptures with the Jehovah's Witnesses
Reasoning from the Scriptures with Masons
Reasoning from the Scriptures with the Mormons
Reasoning from the Scriptures with Muslims

LITTLE BOOKS

Little Book About God
Little Book About Heaven
Little Book About the Bible

AVAILABLE ONLY AS EBOOKS

Book of Bible Promises
Coming Oil Storm
Topical Handbook of Bible Prophecy

Scripture Versions Referenced